E DUE

Cat. No. 23-221

**B**onouring the graduation of

*Daniel Henry Witt*

Class of

**1988**

University of
St. Jerome's College

# Loyalist Mosaic

## A Multi-ethnic Heritage
### by Joan Magee

with contributions by
John S. Dietrich
and
Mary Beacock Fryer
and
a Foreword
by
Charles J. Humber

**Dundurn Press**
Toronto and Charlottetown
1984

## Acknowledgements

The preparation of this manuscript and the publication of this book were made possible because of assistance from several sources. The author wishes to thank Wintario, Ministry of Citizenship and Culture, Government of Ontario. The publisher wishes to acknowledge the ongoing generous financial support of the Canada Council and the Ontario Arts Council.

J. Kirk Howard, Publisher

Editor: Mary Beacock Fryer
Copyeditor: Kevin Bryson
Design and Production: Ron and Ron Design Photography
Typesetting: Q Composition Inc.
Printing and Binding: Marquis Printing, Canada

Published by
**Dundurn Press Limited**
P.O. Box 245, Station F,
Toronto, Canada
M4Y 2L5

## Canadian Cataloguing in Publication Data

Magee, Joan
  Loyalist mosaic

Bibliography: p.
Includes index.
ISBN 0-919670-84-9 (bound). – ISBN 0-919670-85-7 (pbk.)

1. United Empire Loyalists – Biography.*
2. American loyalists – Biography.   I. Title.

FC424.A1M34 1984   971.02′4′0922   C84-099153-3
E277.M34 1984

# Loyalist Mosaic

## A Multi-ethnic Heritage
by Joan Magee

# Contents

# List of Illustrations, Photographs and Maps

# Acknowledgements

The support of the Government of Ontario through the Ministry of Citizenship and Culture, The Honourable Susan Fish, Minister, is acknowledged and greatly appreciated.

The members of the Norden Society of Windsor also wish to express their gratitude to a number of individuals who have contributed to this book with great generosity. Special thanks are due to Eula C. Lapp, author of *To Their Heirs Forever*, now in its third edition, for sharing information about the life and accomplishments of John Dulmage, and thus making an invaluable contribution to this book. In doing so she is sharing in the project of the Norden Society of celebrating the Bicentennial Year, the two hundredth Anniversary of the arrival of the Loyalists in Ontario, through the writing and publication of this book. The Society is also grateful to Mary Beacock Fryer for her assistance both as editor and as contributor of a valuable introductory article on the British military organization of the Loyalist period; to John S. Dietrich for his contribution of a chapter concerning his ancestor James Dittrick, a member of Butler's Rangers; and to Charles J. Humber, President of the United Empire Loyalists' Association of Canada, for his thought-provoking Foreword on the multi-ethnic origins of the Loyalists.

The author also wishes to thank Sheila Wilson, Special Collections, St. Catharines Public Library; Krishna Chandna, Interlibrary Loan Service, Leddy Library, University of Windsor; and Timothy Dubé, Public Archives of Canada, for their assistance in locating important details concerning the life of Richard Pierpoint of St. Catharines.

Members of the Norden Society of Windsor join their President, Evelyn Meyer, Director of the Multicultural Council of Windsor & Essex County, in hoping that *The Loyalist Mosaic* will encourage its readers to develop a fuller understanding of the vital role in Canada's early development played by Loyalists of many ethnic origins.

**J.M.**

# Foreword

Canadian and American students at all levels of education have been taught for far too long that Loyalists of the American Revolution were English. This myth that claims the Loyalists "were British to the core" must today be demythologized if Canadians are ever going to discover their identity.

Those who are knowledgeable about Canadian history agree that tens of thousands of Loyalist refugees were uprooted from their colonial homes during and immediately after the American Revolution. They also concur that many thousands of these exiled refugees evacuated New York City following the 1783 Treaty of Separation and fled to new homes in such distant lands as the Bahamas, the West Indies, Bermuda, East and West Florida, as well as both Nova Scotia and Quebec. Although academics may argue over their numbers, most acknowledge that nearly 7000 exiled Loyalists trekked northwards from upper New York State and the beautiful Mohawk Valley to pioneer in future Ontario where they were relocated along the shores of the upper St. Lawrence and the Bay of Quinte regions during the spring of 1784.

Nevertheless, the myth that these political and war refugees were English "blue-blood" still persists after 200 years. Almost the exact opposite is true, of course. Losers in a bitter civil war, these exiled Americans were as diverse ethnoculturally as they were in their faith, their livelihood and their economic status. To understand and accept these facts is a basic first step toward grasping the elusive Canadian identity.

Inverting the historic telescope and scanning the colonial landscape prior to the outbreak of the American Revolution is one sure way of grasping this fundamental truth that has been misconceptualized over the years.

13

What is today generally called the Delaware Valley or the mid-Atlantic states, namely, New Jersey, eastern Pennsylvania, Delaware and Maryland, had been settled by a very large German mosaic prior to the outbreak of the American Revolution. Until the revolutionaries, or the rebels, became disgruntled with their King, George III, and British Parliament, this large area, first settled massively by William Penn in the late seventeenth century, was dotted with villages, towns and cities named after similar communities of Continental Europe, principally the Rhine River area of central Europe. These Alsatians, Lorraines, Swiss, Flemish, French Huguenots and Palatines in general had maintained their cultural identity for nearly 100 years, many speaking only their native German language in 1775, the year signalling the outbreak of the American Revolution. When this fratricidal war came to an end at Yorktown, Virginia on 17 October 1781, many of these third generation German-speaking settlers fled to British North America as refugee Loyalists. Such names as Eisenhower, Pennypacker, Hoover, Wan[n]amaker, Hershey, Goodyear and Rittenhouse reflect today the powerful influence these German-Americans have had in North America.

New York City, of course, formerly New Amsterdam, had been predominantly Dutch throughout most of the seventeenth century. Areas immediately north of Manhattan, such as New Rochelle, were inhabited by French Huguenots. The further up the Hudson River one went prior to the outbreak of the American Revolution, the more was its multicultural diversity with Dutch, Palatine, Huguenot and various German communities hugging the Hudson River shoreline and its many tributaries. Place names such as Rhinebeck, Poughkeepsie, Hackensack, Fishkill, Peekskill, Nyack and many others scattered throughout the entire area of this historic region suggest that any major English influence there was quite limited, a fact holding true up to the American revolutionary period. Surnames such as Van Cortlandt, Roosevelt, Van Rensselaer, and De Peyster, the latter a prominent Loyalist name, reflect the dominant Dutch influence in the area, while Loyalist surnames such as DeLancey, DeMill[e], Secor[d], Ganong and Mabee, among

14

others, indicate well-known Huguenot names of the same region, especially New Rochelle.

Several of my own Loyalist connections can be traced to this same region. Two of these are the Gunsolos and Emigh families, the former of Spanish origin from Sullivan County, the latter Palatine, from Dutchess County. At the outbreak of the revolutionary war, neither family was English-speaking. Upon their arrival in future Ontario following the American Revolution, both these Loyalist family surnames became "Anglo-Saxonized," the former becoming Consaulous, a prominent Belleville area name during the nineteenth century, the latter Amey. Today, no less than 60 Amey surnames are listed in the Kingston area telephone directories. The 1984 Royal Ontario Museum Bicentennial Exhibition called "Georgian Canada: Conflict and Culture," included Nicholas Amey's Loyalist land grant given to him by his King, George III.

The Mohawk Valley of upper New York State is another major area of colonial America that reflects the dominant ethnic composition of the colonies prior to the American Revolution.

A major group in this region was the Gaelic-speaking Scots Highlanders, perhaps the most influential among those making up the ethnic composition of this region. In addition to the well-known Johnson family, whose roots had been in the Valley for two generations, such well-known Scots as Simon Fraser, the great explorer and for whom the Fraser River in British Columbia is named, could trace their Loyalist ancestry to this area.

Additionally, this beautiful, fertile Valley had a very strong German composition. One famous representative of this ethnocultural group was the Herkimer family that became tragically divided as the result of this fratricidal war.

When the Revolutionary War broke out in 1775, there were perhaps 3,000,000 people living in the colonies. What percentage were non-English is impossible to tell accurately, but a great percentage, more than 50 per cent were of non-British origin, including many Blacks and native Indians. When their property was confiscated, they became refugees. Where they went probably depended on their geographical location. Of the 7,000 or so that made up the "critical mass" that came to future Ontario, there is no question that the English or British element was a minority. The one common denominator that interlinked all of them was their loyalty to the Crown. This book, *The Loyalist Mosaic*, timely published as a bicentennial project of the Norden Society of Windsor should do much to eradicate this old myth that the Loyalists were "British to the core." Joan Magee is to be congratulated for pursuing this myth and putting the Loyalist story into proper perspective. By doing so, she has led us closer to establishing the elusive Canadian identity and has given the next generation a chance to re-discover our roots.

Charles J. Humber, U.E.
National President
The United Empire Loyalists'
    Association of Canada
    (1982-1984)

Portrait of Joseph Brant, *by William Berczy. Joseph Tayada-
neega (Thayendanegea) or Joseph Brant, the great Indian Loyalist
led the greater part of the Mohawks, and a number of Indians
from the other five tribes of the Confederacy of Six Nations,
northwards to Canada.*

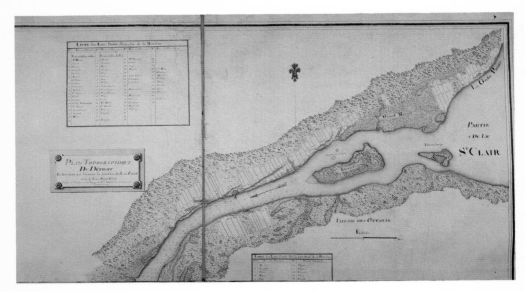

*This map was drawn for potential French military purposes in 1796, and indicates those farms inhabited by French settlers still thought to be loyal to France and likely to give assistance in an eventual American-supported attempt by the French to regain Canada.*

# Chapter One

# The Loyalist Mosaic

The Loyalists whose lives have been considered briefly in the following chapters came from British colonies whose settlers were notable for their variety in religious belief and ethnic origin. While the population figures for the years preceding the first official census of the newly formed United States, taken in 1790, are not considered completely reliable, a fairly accurate estimate has been prepared from various sources.[1] This shows that, quite as one would expect, the immigrants of various ethnic origins coming from Europe tended to group together in the new land, preferring to live near others of a similar background, at least in their first years in America. The origins of the various colonies also led to a predominance of Dutch in certain areas of New York, a former Dutch colony, of Swedes in an area of New Jersey which had been briefly a Swedish colony, and so on. The pattern of settlement of immigrants of different ethnic origins and religions, as of the year 1790 when the official census provided reliable information, can be mapped with real accuracy.

At the outbreak of the American Revolution, fully one-third of the white population of the Thirteen Colonies was of non-English origin. These newcomers were dispersed throughout the colonies, each group tending to establish its own cultural pattern and to retain its mother language, at least for one or two generations.

While the population of New England was chiefly English, the middle colonies included large areas of German, Dutch, and "Scotch-Irish" (Ulster-Protestant) populations. Pennsylvania had three major groups, German, English, and Scotch-Irish, each making up about one-third of the population of the colony. Although English colonists were in the majority in the South, there were large German, Scottish and Scotch-Irish elements in the

19

population, particularly in the frontier areas which had been settled in more recent years.

The Scotch-Irish, the ethnic group to which Henry Magee belonged, made up a sizeable part of the population of the colonies, estimated from between 7 to 17 percent at the beginning of the Revolution. In the peak years, 1771-1775, the time when he emigrated to America, no fewer than 28,000 Scotch-Irish came to America, many of them settling where he did, in the back country frontier areas of Pennsylvania. In fact, in the area where he settled in the Cumberland Valley, the Scotch-Irish made up 90 percent of the population in 1776 when the Revolution broke out.

German-speaking colonists, such as Jacob Dittrick and Peter Etter, made up another ten percent of the total population in 1776. They had settled in Pennsylvania, especially Lancaster County, in large numbers. Many were Swiss and German Mennonites who had fled from persecution in Europe, and were attracted by William Penn's promises of a better life in America. Germans established separate communities in many of the areas of Pennsylvania predominantly settled by the Scotch-Irish. There were large numbers of Germans from the Palatinate who settled in the Mohawk Valley of New York after 1709, some of whom moved to Pennsylvania.

On Sir John Johnson's estate in the Mohawk Valley, there was a sizeable group of Gaelic-speaking Scottish Roman Catholics, and a few Irish Catholics. Most of the Scottish immigrants of the eighteenth century were Highlanders, the majority of whom immigrated between 1763 and 1775, when nearly 25,000 Scots settled in the colonies.

In 1775 the Dutch were still settled in the area which they had originally colonized as New Netherland. They lived along or near the Hudson River, and in New Jersey, where there were many living in Somerset and Bergen counties. Many also lived in New York City or nearby, as did the De Peysters and the Rapeljes. Others had remained in the old Dutch settlements along the Delaware River or moved into pioneering regions of Pennsylvania, as had the Van Dalfsens. Swedes were to be found chiefly in New Jersey and Delaware. The French, however, were scattered throughout the colonies, with Catholic Acadians concentrated in West Florida, and Huguenots in New York, Rhode Island, Pennsylvania, and South Carolina.

In addition, there were small numbers of Italians, Greeks, and Minorcans in Florida, a few Welsh in distinctive settlements, and some Norwegians who lived in Swedish communities in Delaware.

Blacks formed 20 percent of the total population, and of these 8 percent were free and 12 percent lived in slavery. They were found in all the colonies as were the native Indians.

The colony of New York, from which so many of the Loyalists came, was particularly varied in the ethnic make-up of its population. This did not please some Englishmen who were used to a more homogenous population in England. In 1692 one remarked: "Our chiefest unhappyness is too great a mixture of nations."[2] In 1760 another one wrote, "Being . . . of different nations, different languages, and different religions, it is almost impossible to give them [New Yorkers] any precise or determinate character."[3]

This great complexity began with the colonization carried out by the Dutch. As far as the West Indian Company was concerned, in their colony of New Netherland, Lutherans, Jews, and Quakers need not conform and worship with the religious majority in the Reformed Church:

> At least not force people's conscience, but allow everyone to have his own belief, as long as he behaves quietly and legally, gives no offence to his neighbours, and does not oppose the government.[4]

As a result of this broad tolerance, which reflected the attitude prevalent in the Netherlands itself, there was no attempt to convert those of other faiths to the Reformed religion.

Although the language of New Netherland was Dutch, the colonists were by no means all of "Dutch origin." This has been proven by an American historian, Oliver A. Rink, who recently analysed original sources in the Netherlands and the United States to determine the ethnic background of immigrants who came to New Netherland

21

in the seventeenth century, and whose descendants formed the "Dutch" ethnic group in New York at the time of the outbreak of the American Revolution. He discovered that the first colonists to arrive were Walloon refugees fleeing the Spanish in the Southern Netherlands, or present-day Belgium. They described themselves as "diverse families of all manner of manufacture who, having solicited the English to be transported to Virginia, would now prefer to be employed by the West India Company."[5]

This group was followed by other shiploads of settlers, many of them refugees from war-torn European countries. In an analysis of the ethnic origins of 904 immigrants to New Netherland, Rink discovered that while 50.8 percent were originally from the Netherlands itself, others came from many different countries: Spanish Netherlands, seven percent; Germany (a number of independent German states), eighteen percent; France, seven percent; Schleswig-Holstein, seven percent; Denmark, one percent; Sweden, three percent; Norway, five percent; others, one percent, including, surprisingly, three individuals from Poland.[6]

A generation later, these immigrants to New Netherland were integrated into a Dutch-speaking community, one which may well have seemed uniformly Dutch to the English when they captured the colony in 1664 and brought to it the English language and the Anglican church. In light of the above information about the origin of the New Netherlanders, it is not surprising to learn that the Loyalist Van Buskirk family was of part-Dutch, part-Danish origin, or that the Rapeljes had French Huguenot and Dutch roots.

The Loyalists came from various parts of the Thirteen Colonies to enter a sparsely populated wilderness. In the whole of Canada, there were only about 123,000 persons, excluding the Indians. Nova Scotia then included the area which is now known as New Brunswick, and had fewer than 20,000 people, living for the most part along the coastal regions and on the St. John River. The majority were American-born of English colonial stock, but there were about 9,000 Acadians, some Scots, and some "foreign Protestants," mainly German and Swiss. Quebec, which included present-day Ontario, had a population of approximately 90,000 almost all of whom were French in origin, and Roman Catholic. Except for a few people living at military posts such as Detroit, there were no large settlements west of Montreal. In fact, in the area that is now southern Ontario, there were only some 20,000 Indians, the remnants of a larger population which had been wiped out in tribal wars, and about 660 French settlers in which is now Essex county, across from Detroit. Detroit, as a whole, had about 1,500 residents, mostly French in origin, but with a number of settlers, as well as the military, of British and Dutch origin. The one-third who lived on what is now the Canadian side of the river were all French. These were families from Detroit who had established long, ribbon-shaped farms on the south and east shores of the Detroit River according to a regular plan of settlement 1749-1751, making this area the oldest continuously settled agricultural area in the Province of Ontario. (Thus, already in 1949 the local French Canadian population of this area of Ontario were able to celebrate 200 years of residence in this province.)

The Loyalists, beginning in 1784 and continuing for some years, were assigned lands in this sparsely settled wilderness by Governor Frederick Haldimand, himself a French-speaking Swiss of Huguenot origin. They were settled in groups of families and friends and comrades-in-arms from the Loyalists' disbanded regiments. Once again, as had been the case in their former homes to the south, there was a tendency to form new settlements with others of the same ethnic origin. This has been noted by many observers, among them the investigators for an Ethnological Survey of Canada, taken at the end of the past century:

It has often been observed that in Ontario, as well as in almost every other new colony, the early settlers located, as a rule, in groups or clusters according to nationality or religious creed. In the course of a journey through the province one comes upon groups of English, Scots, Irish, French, Germans, etc. The particular nationality or creed in each case determines the characteristic traits of the group – traits which persist through several generations, notwithstanding the levelling tendencies of modern life.[7]

23

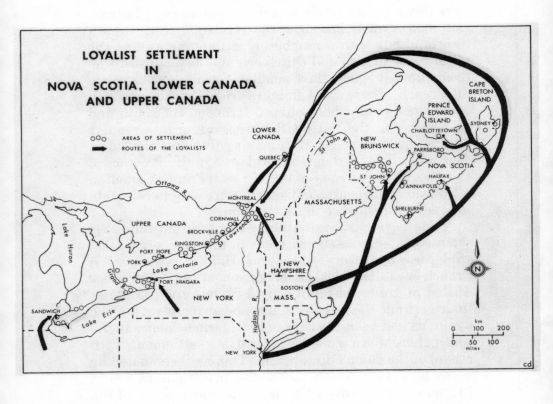

LOYALIST SETTLEMENT
IN
NOVA SCOTIA, LOWER CANADA
AND UPPER CANADA

ooo  AREAS OF SETTLEMENT
→  ROUTES OF THE LOYALISTS

A map showing the movement of Loyalists north-ward to their new homes in Canada gives a strong in-dication of the nature of the ethnic communities that were established. For example, it would appear that Loyalists from the Mohawk Valley and Hudson River Valley would tend to found Mohawk Indian, Palatine German, and Dutch communities. This did indeed occur, although, of course, there was a degree of intermixture of ethnic groups in some of the new settlements, particularly in areas settled by regiments which had included soldiers of varied ethnic origins.

The largest ethnic group of Loyalists to settle in Upper Canada was the German.[8] They came chiefly from New York and Pennsylvania, and settled mainly in Stor-mont, Dundas, Lennox and Addington, and Prince Ed-ward counties, although many were found in smaller numbers in other Loyalist settlements in Upper Canada.

The Dutch settled chiefly in Stormont, Dundas, Len-nox and Addington, and in the Niagara and Long Point areas. Some who had both Dutch and German Palatine origins and came from New York State settled together in the townships of Ernestown, Adolphustown, Freder-ickburgh, and Richmond, near the Bay of Quinte.

Highland Scots, Roman Catholic tenants from the estate of Sir John Johnson in the Mohawk Valley, had fought in their landlord-chief's King's Royal Regiment of New York. They were settled together in Glengarry County after the war.

In 1784 two major groups of Indians of the Confed-eracy of the Six Nations settled in Upper Canada, while a small third group remained behind in the Mohawk Val-ley where they were of assistance to the British in the years following the end of the Revolution. One group of Mohawks led by John Deseronto, settled at Tyendinaga, in the Bay of Quinte area. A much larger group, under Joseph Brant, settled temporarily in the Niagara Pen-insula and then moved to a grant of land along the banks of the Grand River.

The Blacks represented about ten percent of the Loy-alists in Nova Scotia. They settled in groups, with about 200 going to the St. John River area, 400 living in Halifax, 200 moving to Digby, and the great majority remaining

25

in Shelburne in a black area called Birchtown. In Upper Canada, there were a few black Loyalists, some of whom had served in the various Loyalist regiments. Nineteen Blacks signed a petition asking for the right to establish their own all-black community, but this was not answered in the affirmative.

It can be seen that it is certainly a myth that the Loyalists tended to be wealthy, Anglican, and of English origin. A few had been wealthy, some were Anglican, and many, particularly in the Maritimes, were of English origin. At the same time, many Germans joined the New Jersey Volunteers, possibly the largest Loyalist regiment, and were resettled in the Maritimes. The ancestor of the late John Fisher – "Mr. Canada" – was Ludwig Fischer of that regiment.

The Loyalists represented a cross-section of the society which they had left behind them. They represented all parts of this society, and in their midst included farmers, craftsmen, tradesmen, officials, Indians, slaves and former slaves. Many of those who came to Upper Canada were pioneer farmers in the newly developing regions of the frontier country of Pennsylvania and New York.

Speaking many languages, worshipping in many different ways, the Loyalists arrived in the unpopulated wilderness of Ontario 200 years ago. In doing so, they founded our multicultural society of today.

*A Loyalist of French Canadian origin, Jacques Duperron (James) Bâby (1762-1833) was born at Detroit. His family was staunchly loyal to the British Crown during the American Revolution and was forced to move across the Detroit River to the Canadian side about 1789. In 1792 he was appointed a member of the Executive and Legislative Councils of Upper Canada and continued to sit on these councils until his death.*

*When the Bâby family moved to the Canadian side of the Detroit River as Loyalists, they first lived in a small cabin on the banks of the river. Later James Bâby bought this fine house not far from the original cabin.*

# Chapter Two

# The British Military Organization 1775–1784

By Mary Beacock Fryer

During the American Revolution, thousands of men in Britain's North American colonies enlisted in what were called Provincial Corps of the British Army, which were similar to numbered British regular regiments of foot. The more popular name for a Provincial Corps was Loyalist regiment. Corps of Provincial troops were based wherever the British regular army was in control, and they took part in many expeditions and raids into the parts of the American colonies that were controlled by the rebels. Some understanding of the military organization, and the geography of the British-controlled areas, is essential if the experiences of the individual Loyalists recounted in subsequent chapters are to be viewed in the proper context.

Early in the revolution, Britain established four secure bases, difficult for the American rebels to assail, that were known as military departments. The largest, and the most strategic, was the Central Department in and around New York City – Manhattan, Staten and Long Islands – which the British occupied in the autumn of 1776 and did not evacuate completely until November 1783, more than two months after the final peace treaty was signed on 8 September. The Southern Department was East and West Florida, with headquarters in St. Augustine.[1] The Eastern (or Northeastern) Department was Nova Scotia (which then included New Brunswick) with headquarters in Halifax.

The Northern Department was the Province of Quebec (now Quebec and Ontario) with headquarters in Quebec City. At the same time, Montreal, close to the invasion route down Lake Champlain and the Richelieu River, was also of strategic importance. The Northern Department was threatened in the autumn of 1775. A rebel army advanced from Lake Champlain and occupied Montreal, while another, travelling by way of the Kennebec River from what is now Maine and down the Chaudière River, attacked Quebec City. The goal of both thrusts was the capture of Quebec. The occupation lasted until the spring of 1776, when a fleet from Britain brought reinforcements and the rebels withdrew up Lake Champlain. Afterwards the Northern Department was secure.

At each military department, British regular troops were stationed. As well, all except the Southern Department were reinforced by German regiments rented by George III, as elector of Hanover, from his various dependencies. Disparagingly called "Hessian mercenaries" in American sources, these soldiers were members of established German regiments. They were not mercenaries in the usual sense of the word, for they were George III's own troops.

Attached to each military department were Provincial Corps of the British Army, special regiments established for the duration of the war, in which loyal colonials served. To each departmental headquarters came Loyalists, some to enlist as Provincials, others in search of a safe haven where they could find employment, often in essential work, in order to earn a living until peace was restored. To each department, too, came refugee families – women and children sometimes accompanying the head of the family. Sometimes they came on their own to join husbands and fathers who had been forced to flee. The latter left their families at home in the hope that they could carry on for the duration of the war, optimistic that Britain would soon restore order.[2]

Some refugees made their escape to places that the British army occupied temporarily, and the men often provided needed reinforcements to the Provincial Corps that accompanied the regulars. Early in the war some went to Boston, where the army had been sent to quell disturbances in Massachusetts. When, in March 1776, rebel

30

pressure forced the British to evacuate Boston and retire to Halifax, many refugees who had sought protection there left with the army. Philadelphia was occupied by the British from September 1777 until June 1778, and again, when the army withdrew to New York City, many refugees went along. Similarly, when the British abandoned Savannah, Georgia, in July 1782, and Charleston, South Carolina, in December of that year, more refugees went along and were sheltered in and around New York City.

A far greater number of refugees, however, escaped persecution by reaching one of the four military departments on their own. The largest proportion found their way to the headquarters of the Central Department at New York City. This department was the most convenient to reach, and had more resources for the care of the refugees than the other military departments had. Agriculture was more productive, the port of New York was ice-free year-round for the British supply fleets, and wealthy individuals were able to contribute to Loyalist relief, alleviating some of the burden placed on the British government.[3] Nevertheless, the British-occupied area around New York became crowded, and food and firewood sometimes fell far short of the demand. While the largest number of Provincial Corps operated from the Central Department, the area around New York City had a higher proportion of civilian refugees than were sheltered in the other departments. Many of the men were able to find civilian employment, although they were part-time soldiers in the militia, as opposed to full-time service in one of the Provincial Corps.

As already stated, some refugees reached Nova Scotia early in the war. However, the main exodus to Nova Scotia, amounting to between 30,000 and 40,000 people, began with the sailing of the "Spring Fleet" from New York City on 26 April 1783. Sent to Nova Scotia were Provincials of the Central Department who were disbanded soon after they arrived, British regulars who wished to settle there because their regiments were being reduced, and the many civilians. For the journey, men who had not been in Provincial Corps were organized into militia companies under specially appointed officers, and accompanied by their dependents. Though in militia companies, these men were

*A Butler's Rangers button found at the Matthew Elliott Site, Amherstburg, Ontario.*

still civilians and did not have the same status as disbanded Provincials and regulars. The specially appointed officers, for example, were not entitled to receive half-pay, while Provincial and regular officers were. In the traditions of the Maritime provinces, a distinction is drawn between disbanded soldiers and Loyalists, although soldiers who had been in Provincial Corps were Loyalists as well.

Conditions in the Northern Department were somewhat different from those at New York City and later Nova Scotia. The supply situation was much more restrictive because the French Canadian farms did not yield a large surplus, and the troops and refugees were more dependent on the supply fleets sent from Britain. Furthermore, the port of Quebec was icebound for part of the year, and the supply fleets were often delayed. As a consequence, General Frederick Haldimand, a Swiss professional soldier in Britain's service who was the Governor of Canada from June 1778 until after the war, scattered the troops stationed along the lower St. Lawrence River in small contingents. That way, they were less likely to exhaust the local food supply beyond its limits. Supplying his troops in the western wilderness, such as Butler's Rangers who were stationed at Niagara, posed a more serious problem. Not only did supplies for the troops have to be transported from Montreal, but some refugees, both Loyalist and Indian, sought shelter at Fort Niagara. In 1781, Haldimand struck a bargain with the Mississauga Indians, who sold a strip of land to the government for an agricultural settlement (the site of Niagara-on-the-Lake).

Haldimand also insisted that anyone receiving government assistance should contribute to the war effort, with the exception of women with young children, the elderly and the infirm. All able-bodied men and older boys were almost forced to enlist in Provincial Corps – including some who were brought into Quebec as prisoners-of-war, provided that someone could vouch that they had Loyalist sympathies. Many prisoners were able to prove, to the governor's satisfaction, that they had been coerced into serving with the rebels in the first place. Haldimand also sent back to the rebelling colonies American resi-

*Detail of the United Empire Loyalist Memorial Window, Grace United Church, Napanee, Ontario.*

Bishop Alexander Macdonell *(1760-1840). This illustrious and capable Highland Scottish clergyman took over charge of the Roman Catholic parish of New Johnstown (Cornwall, Ontario) in October 1804, replacing Rev. Joachim Roderick Macdonell (1756-1806), a Gaelic-speaking priest who ministered to the Scottish Loyalists from 1778 to 1804, and Rev. Alexander ("Scotus") Macdonell (c1740-1803), a missionary priest. They were all fluent in Scots Gaelic, and native to the Highlands of Western Scotland.*

dents of Montreal and their dependents if their loyalties were in question, to ease the strain on available supplies.

Women who did not have small children, and many daughters of Loyalists, were assigned to the various frontier posts where their men were on duty, to do the housekeeping chores. They were provisioned or paid a pittance towards their keep. When the war ended, very few male Loyalists in Quebec were civilians. Nearly all heads of families and single men were former Provincials. The exceptions were reduced British and German regulars who wanted to remain as settlers, and two small groups of civilians, organized into militia companies, from New York City. Led by Michael Grass and Peter van Alstyne, they preferred settling in Quebec over Nova Scotia. Thus, unlike the much larger migration to Nova Scotia, with its substantial civilian component, the founders of Ontario were generally military men and their dependents who had endured as many as seven years of war.

Most of the 7,000 to 8,000 Loyalists who were in Quebec were resettled in the western wilderness (now Ontario) in 1784. In deciding to locate his Loyalists well away from the seigneuries of the French-Canadians, Haldimand recognized the vast cultural gap that existed between the King's French-speaking Roman Catholic subjects and the Loyalists. Because of the Loyalists' military background, he settled them by regiments, assigning the required number of townships to each. Within the townships he encouraged the various language and religious groups to settle together. For instance, he placed Gaelic-speaking Scots Highlanders who were Roman Catholic closest to the most westerly seigneury, with the Protestant Loyalists farther West. In his desire to have the different cultural groups live among their own kind, the governor, himself a French-speaking Huguenot from a multilingual country, showed his awareness that his Loyalists were a mosaic of cultures. He seemed to have anticipated that Canada was not destined to become a "melting pot."

# Chapter Three

## Arent Schuyler de Peyster
## (1736–1822)
## A Dutchman on
## Canada's Frontier

*De Peyster was "Anglican and wealthy," but he was not of English descent. Strictly speaking he cannot be said to be Dutch, for he was a native-born American. But his family came to America from the Northern Netherlands, and his ancestors originally came from Flanders. He was of Dutch and Flemish origin, and raised in the Dutch community of New York, formerly New Amsterdam.*

Arent Schuyler De Peyster arrived in the Detroit River area in 1779, not to settle but to serve as the British commandant of Detroit, then an important outpost of British North America. Of Dutch descent, this American-born British citizen was to have a lasting influence on the settlement, and his service with the British army saw him rise to colonel of his regiment – the 8th, or King's Regiment of Foot, with headquarters in Liverpool, England; an unusual achievement. Instances of a colonial reaching so high a rank in the regular army were very rare.

De Peyster was raised in New York City when some still lived who could remember it as New Amsterdam, capital of the Dutch colony of New Netherland. Born on 27 June 1736, he was the son of Pierre Guillaume De Peyster (Peter De Peyster) and Cornelia Schuyler, daughter of Arent Schuyler and his second wife, Swantje Dyckhuyse. The Christian names "Pierre Guillame" may be traced for generations in the De Peyster family to their city of origin, Ghent, in what is now Belgium, but was then the Southern Netherlands.

In 1566, during the Netherlands' great struggle for independence from Spain, the De Peysters became Prot-

37

*As an officer in the British regular army Arent Schuyler De Peyster, a descendant of early settlers of New Netherland, played a prominent role in maintaining both military and civil control for the British during the years 1765-1785.*

Hier siet gy dat Paleys dat Willem Graef en koning    Nu is het Raed-huys hier daer van der Stede wegen    Hoe kan een Land bestaen, al waer de goede eeden
Heeft tot syn Hof gesticht, en Koninklyke woning'    De Raeden besig syn om goeden eaed te pleegen    Al waer der Wetten-tucht met roetehyp als getret?
Gelyk soo voor als na het Graeflyke Hof    Daert recht gewesen werd wanneer der twist ontstaet,    Gelykerwys de ziel het lyf is slevens band?
Te Haerlem is geweest tot onzer eer en lof    En daer die word gestraft diesich te buytengaet:    So is gerechtigheyt het leven van een Land.

*The market place of Haarlem as viewed in this etching would
have been familiar to Jean de Peyster, the immigrant ancestor
of Arent Schuyler De Peyster, who left Haarlem for New
Amsterdam around 1645.*

estants, and the long family migrations began. At first, the De Peyster family, together with other Protestants from Ghent, fled to Haarlem, in the Northern Netherlands[1] where their names are found on the registers of Flemish Protestant churches after 1570. However, after 1579, they had to return to Ghent and pay fines for not having obtained permission from the magistrates to leave that city. Some left once again, but Arent De Peyster's branch stayed in Ghent for some years. One of his ancestors was born there in 1595, but eventually made his way to Haarlem, where he died in 1648. This ancestor's son, Jean De Peyster, born in Haarlem in 1626, emigrated in about the year 1645 to New Amsterdam with other Flemish Protestants, Huguenots, and Walloons.

Such religious refugees made up a considerable portion of the number of immigrants who went to New Netherland, for they were already uprooted and looked for economic opportunity in the New World. Though considered nobility in the Netherlands, the De Peysters were also refugees, and had to resort to trade to earn a living.

Once in New Amsterdam, the De Peysters became one of the prominent families of the colony, with connections by marriage to many of the *patroon* families, the great landowners of New Netherland. One of these was the Schuyler family, founded by Philip Pietersen Schuyler of Amsterdam, of which Arent Schuyler De Peyster's mother was a member. Her brother became a colonel in the British army, following the Schuyler family's long tradition of military participation wherever they lived.

At the time of the capitulation of New Netherland to the British, the total white population has been estimated at between eight and ten thousand, about two-thirds of whom were Dutch. The majority, including the De Peysters, stayed after the English took over the colony. As a result, not only did Dutch culture survive in New York and New Jersey – it blossomed – and it is recognized that the greatest strides in the development of Dutch cultural life occurred not before, but after the English came to power.[2] The De Peysters, like other former Dutch colonists, had little difficulty adjusting to English rule. In fact, the family became ardent supporters of the English, and several members, including Arent De

*The De Peyster family lived in this imposing home on Pearl Street in New York City.*

Peyster's father, had distinguished careers in the British army.

When Arent was born in 1736, the Dutch language was still in daily use in New York among those of Dutch background. The Reformed Church, to which the family had belonged for generations, held its service in Dutch, and continued to be responsible to the *classis*[3] of Amsterdam. An agreement had been made, more than 30 years after the English had taken the colony, that the Dutch Reformed Church (later to become the Reformed Church of America) could continue to work and to hold services without interference. The church also maintained schools in which the language of instruction was Dutch.

His father, perhaps influenced by his career in the British army, had left the Dutch Reformed Church, becoming an Anglican by the time of his marriage to Swantje Dyckhuyse. They were married as Anglicans and Arent De Peyster was brought up in that church. It is not surprising, therefore, that his Dutch origins were seldom mentioned. In fact, he is frequently incorrectly said to have been of Huguenot ancestry. This error is perhaps due to the French Christian names traditional in the family.

Arent De Peyster followed his father's example in choosing a military career, and in 1755 he was commissioned third lieutenant in the Independent Company of Grenadiers of the City of New York. Later, he transferred to the 8th (King's) Regiment, and following the end of hostilities in the colonies (during the Seven Years' War) he was posted to Ireland and Germany, returning to North America in 1768. While he was overseas, he married Rebecca Blair, a Scotswoman whose home was Mavis Hall, near Dumfries.

Six years later, with the threat of revolution hanging over the English colonies, his regiment was sent to garrison the strategic forts at Niagara, Detroit, and Michilimackinac. The regimental headquarters were actually in Montreal, but about 100 men were assigned to each of these vitally important frontier outposts.

As the American Revolution began and the American colonists were forced to side with either the rebels or

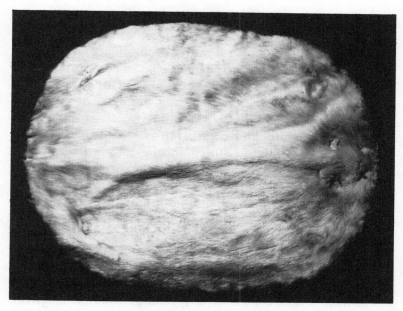

*White beaver pelt of the evil spirit that nearly caused De Peyster's death at the hand of a "possessed" Indian brave at Michilimackinac.*

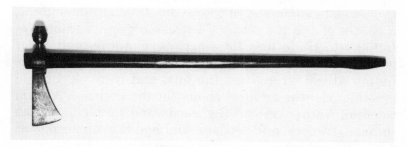

*Tomahawk from Colonel De Peyster's collection of Indian artifacts collected during his years of army service in America.*

the Loyalists, Arent De Peyster chose to support the King. This was not necessarily a foregone conclusion, for in the De Peyster family, as in so many other colonial families, there were supporters for both sides, the reason for their choice varying from person to person. However, many Dutchmen in New York remained neutral despite the pressure to choose sides. This choice was scarcely open to Arent De Peyster in his position as a professional military man. His cousin, Philip John Schuyler, became a major-general in the Revolutionary Army, leading the war against the Loyalists in upper New York State. But De Peyster, coming from the same background of generations of wealthy Dutch landowners and merchants, remained loyal. That it was not simple expediency but a sincere choice, made from lifelong personal loyalty to the British government, is shown by his letters and statements made by him and about him during his life. Even his obituary made note of the strength of his political principles, "firm even to inflexibility." So, in the years immediately preceding the American Revolution, there is no doubt that Arent De Peyster continued to serve as a British officer with unwavering loyalty in spite of the defections he observed about him.

For five years, 1774-1779, De Peyster, by now a captain, was in command of the troops at Michilimackinac, a centre of the fur trade. To it came great numbers of Indians to trade furs for weapons, clothing, and other goods. De Peyster's role was to keep the goodwill of the Indian allies, strengthen the fort, and increase British prestige. He was an ideal choice for the position. A loyal colonial, he understood the needs and problems of the Indians, traders, and settlers, and had the advantage as well of an upbringing in a prominent military family with English sympathies.

While De Peyster was at Michilimackinac, one of the most memorable incidents of his long and colourful career occurred. An Indian was caught lurking about the Fort in a suspicious manner. When questioned, he admitted he had intended to kill the commandant, Captain De Peyster. Further interrogation made him admit he was following the orders of a powerful evil spirit which had taken the form of a large white beaver. The Indian agreed that it was wrong to seek De Peyster's life, but insisted he must obey the spirit's command. After much effort, he was persuaded to kill the spirit instead of the commandant. Armed with weapons supplied by the garrison, the Indian set out to hunt. Some time later, he returned with the pelt of a pure white beaver. De Peyster kept the skin as a souvenir of the incident, and it eventually wound up in his home in Scotland.[4]

After five years in Michilimackinac, De Peyster was promoted to major and made commandant of Detroit. In 1779 he came down from the north by boat to replace the former commandant, Henry Hamilton, who had been captured by the rebels.[5]

Soon after his arrival, De Peyster set teams of men to work building a more modern British fort to replace the old French fortifications. The new one, known as Fort Lernoult (eventually renamed Fort Shelby when Detroit passed to the United States in 1796), was to be on higher ground back of the old palisaded French village which had been founded by Cadillac in 1701, and populated with disbanded French soldiers and their families.

Though De Peyster remained in Detroit for only five years, his influence on the border regions was of lasting importance. He was a close friend of fur-trader John Askin, who himself was a writer of many letters important for the understanding of the early history of the region — papers which have been collected and published under the title *The John Askin Papers*.[6]

While there is no evidence that Arent made use of his mother tongue during his years of service in Detroit, it is quite possible that he did do so, since it is known that he spoke it. He would have found his knowledge of the language useful in dealing with the Moravians and their Indian converts, who spoke a form of Low German not unlike Dutch, and with Dutch-speaking settlers among the Loyalist refugees from the states of New York, New Jersey, and Pennsylvania. However, English was his main language throughout his life, though he could also speak and write French with great fluency, an ability very important in Detroit.

Of the many orders, documents and letters written by De Peyster, a large number have been preserved,

45

including some exchanged by Askin and De Peyster and found in the *Papers*. De Peyster had known Askin at Michilimackinac where Askin had worked in the British military post as well as traded in furs and Indian goods. Askin arrived in Detroit in 1780 and spent 22 years there. When Detroit was handed over to the United States in 1796, its citizens were given a choice between British and American citizenship. Askin chose to remain British, though he stayed in Detroit for some years longer, before moving across the river to Sandwich. Throughout the period he continued to correspond with De Peyster, who remained a close friend, and never forgot the ties he made in Detroit.

In his Scottish country home near Dumfries where he lived after the revolution, De Peyster kept a collection of souvenirs of his military career in America, many of them Indian items, including snowshoes, moccasins, four peace pipes, legties, wrist and head bands, a tomahawk, a wampum "belt of alliance", and a Sioux skin pouch, all from the Michilimackinac and Detroit River region. These items have been carefully preserved and are now in the collection of the Liverpool Museum.

De Peyster's friendship with the Indians and real concern about their problems led to one important development in local history. As commandant of Detroit, he ordered a group of Moravians to leave their settlement near Pittsburgh and move to Detroit.

This orderly, peaceful colony of Delaware Indian converts, established by the Moravians, lived in a district made dangerous by roving bands of warlike Indians as well as white settlers seeking revenge for Indian raids. The Moravian missionaries had become caught up in the revolution through unfortunate circumstances. They had issued a note of warning to the Americans, solely as a benevolent act. This act had managed, however, to anger the British, who tried to break up the missions and remove the missionaries from their converts. Orders thus came from De Peyster that the missionaries should appear in Detroit to answer to charges of "meddling with Public Matters."[7] Virtual prisoners, the Moravian group, led by David Zeisberger, travelled to judgement. Their trip led through the wilderness to Detroit, passing Wyandotte settlements and French Canadian "ribbon farms" whose houses, facing the water, Zeisberger described as sitting close together "like a village along the river."[8] The historian, Elma Gray, in her book about the Moravian mission to the Delaware Indians, has provided a vivid description of the Detroit waterfront as it must have appeared to Zeisberger and his companions:

> Between the two banks, one-half mile apart, flowed 'the strait' Detroit, conveying to Lake Erie all the waters of the Upper Lakes. Borne on its current, with all the beauty of white sails, were the navy sloops and the merchant vessels.
> From the loading dock and landing place below the fort, two-wheeled carts, drawn by small French horses, or ponies, brought the cargoes to the top, handled by noisy, jovial Frenchmen. . . . Such was Detroit in 1701, when Cadillac landed, until 1760, when it became the seat of British western authority. . . . The [Moravian] travelers, halted at the drawbridge, had time to say a short prayer and square their shoulders before they were led through the gate, across narrow streets to the eastern edge of the fort, to the home of Major De Peyster.[9]

Once in Detroit, De Peyster questioned the Moravians closely as to the reasons for their behaviour. Convinced they had been acting in charity rather than "meddling with Public Matters," he publicly declared them free to return to their camping grounds at Sandusky. From that point on, De Peyster and the Moravians were friends. The commandant supplied them with clothes for themselves and their families and gave them fresh horses, for theirs had been stolen in Detroit. He also gave them supplies, for they were dangerously close to starvation and, most important of all, a passport permitting them to "perform the functions of their [office] among the Christian Indians without molestation".[10] At first, the group camped in a temporary location on the Clinton River north of Detroit, but later, with the help of De Peyster, they were given land closer to the fort.

Although by 1784 De Peyster had left Detroit, he had become a close friend of David Zeisberger and his Indian followers, and continued to take a strong interest in their welfare, obtaining news through his correspondence with his many friends in the Detroit area. He wrote to Askin:

> Dumfries 11th March 1804
> My dear Askin: Your friendly letter from near Sandwich opposite Hog Island,[11] without a date, is truly flattering as it convinces both Mrs. D and myself that you are that steady friend I always supposed you would prove, for it is time alone which is the true touchstone of friendship.... My old Indian friends, the Chiefs I mean, I hear are mostly dead, Particularly Quiouigoushquin and Moneso[12] Bennet's fr[i]end Matchiquis. If Wawayachterin the Pottawatomie is living and you see him, tell him that I have not forgot him nor any of my Huron friends.[13]

In June 1784, De Peyster was promoted lieutenant-colonel of the 8th Regiment, and posted to Fort Niagara, the headquarters of the British Indian Department. He was then the senior commander for all the British forts above Montreal. The following year he moved to England and was stationed at Portsmouth, where he corresponded with John Askin, still at Detroit. In 1795, after 40 years of service, he retired from the British army and went to Dumfries to live in Mavis Hall, the country seat which had belonged to his wife's family for many years. However, he was soon recalled to service due to Napoleon's threatened invasion of England. He was placed in charge of the Gentlemen Volunteers of Dumfries, who numbered the famous poet, Robert Burns, as one of their company.[14] The two men exchanged poems, for De Peyster was an amateur poet of some talent. A poem De Peyster wrote while commandant at Detroit illustrates his gift:

Red River

*A song, descriptive of the diversion of carioling*
*or staying upon the Ice at the Post of Detroit,*
*in North America*
*Tune — The Banks of the Dee*

In winter, when rivers and lakes do cease flowing,

The Limnades (Lake Nymphs) to warm shelter all
    fled;
When ships are unrigged, and their boats do cease
    rowing,
'Tis then we drive up and down sweet River Red.
Freeze River Red, sweet serpentine river,
    Where swift carioling[1] is dear to me ever;
While frost-bound, the *Dunmore*, the *Gage*, and *En-
    deavour*,[2]
    Your ice bears me on to a *croupe en grillade*.

Our bodies wrapped up in a robe lined with sable,
    A mask o'er the face, and fur cap on the head,
We drive out to dinner – where there is no table,
    No chairs we can sit on, or stools in their stead.
Freeze River Red, sweet serpentine river,
    Where sweet carioling is dear to me ever;
To woods, where on bear skins, we sit down so clever,
    While served by the *Marqui*[4] with *croupe en gril-
    lade*.

'*Une Verre de Madeir*,' with his aspect so pleasing,
    He serves to each lady (who takes it in turn)
And says, *Chere Madame, dis will keep you* from
    freezing,
    *Was* warm you within where the fire it would burn.
Freeze River Red, sweet serpentine river,
    For your carioling is dear to me ever;
Where served by the *Marquis* so polite and clever,
    With smiles, and Madeir, and a *croupe en grillade*.

The goblet goes round, while sweet echo's repeating
    The words which have passed through each fair
    lady's lips;
Wild deer (with projected long ears) leave off eating,
    And bears sit attentive, erect on their hips.
Freeze River Red, sweet serpentine river,
    Your fine wooded banks shall be dear to me ever,
Where echo repeats Madame's *Chançon* so clever,
    Distinctly you hear it say *croupe-en-grillade*.

The fort gun proclaims when 'tis time for returning,
    Our pacers all eager at home to be fed;
We leave all the fragments, and wood clove for burn-
    ing,
    For those who may next drive up sweet River Red.
Freeze River Red, sweet serpentine river,

49

On you, carioling, be dear to me ever,
Where wit and good humor were ne'er known to sever,
   While drinking a glass to a *croupe en grillade*.

   [1] The cariole is generally drawn by a fast pacing horse.
   [2] Three ships-of-war upon the lakes.
   [3] A French name for a *barbecued* rump of vension.
   [4] The Marquis was the most obliging man living. He was a captain
      in the Indian department, and had all the French old-school in
      his manners. His name was La Motte, and he spoke a peculiar
      sort of English.[15]

With a common interest in poetry, De Peyster and
Burns became close friends. Tragically, however, Burns
became very ill while serving in the Volunteers in the
spring of 1796, and in April he wrote:

Almost ever since I wrote you last, I have only known
Existence by the pressure of the heavy hand of Sickness; & have counted time by the repercussion of
PAIN! Rheumatism, Cold, & Fever had formed, to me,
a terrible Trinity in Unity, which makes me close
my eyes in misery, & open them without hope.[16]

Although gravely ill, Burns wrote a poem at this
time, the last which he was to write, for he died later
that same year. He addressed this poem to his friend,
Colonel De Peyster, thanking De Peyster for the kindness
shown during his illness:

Poem on Life

*Addressed to Colonel De Peyster, Dumfries, 1796*

   My honored colonel, deep I feel
Your interest in the Poet's weal; Ah! now sma' heart
      hae I to speel
   The steep Parnassus,
Surrounded thus by bolus pill,
      And potion glasses.

O what a canty warld were it,
Would pain and care, and sickness spare it;
And fortune favor worth and merit,
      As they deserve:

50

(And aye a rowth, roast beef and claret;
    Syne wha would starve?)

Dame life, tho' fiction out may trick her,
And in paste gems and frippery deck her;
Oh! flickering, feeble, and unsicker
    I've found her still,
Ay wavering like the willow wicker,
    'Tween good and ill.

Then that crust carmagnole, auld Satan,
Watches, like bawd'rons by a rattan,
Our sinfu' saul to get a claute on
    Wi' felon ire;
Syne, whip! his tail ye'll ne'er cast saut on,
    He's off like fire.

Ah! Nick, ah Nick it is na fair,
First shewing us the tempting ware,
Bright wines and bonnie lasses rare,
    To put us daft;
Syne weave, unseen, thy spider snare
    O' hell's damned waft.

Poor man the flie, aft bizzes bye,
And aft as chance he comes thee nigh,
They auld damned elbow yeuks wi' joy,
    And hellish pleasure;
Already in thy fancy's eye,
    Thy sicker treasure.

Soon heels o'er gowdie! in he gangs,
And like a sheep-head on a tangs,
Thy girning laugh enjoys his pangs
    And murdering wrestle,
As dangling in the wind he hangs
    A gibbet's tassel.

But lest you think I am uncivil,
To plague you with this draunting drivel,
Abjuring a' intentions evil,
    I quat my pen:
The Lord Preserve us frae the devil!
    Amen! Amen![17]

Arent De Peyster outlived his friend Robert Burns
by many years, reaching the age of 86 before he died on
26 November 1822. By that time, he had held the royal

*Arent Schuyler De Peyster spent the last years of his life in retirement at Mavis Grove, the home near Dumfries, Scotland, which his wife had inherited from her family.*

commission for more than 60 years. He was buried next to Burns, in the cemetery of St. Michael's Church in Dumfries, on 2 December 1822, with full military honours. An obituary printed in the local paper at the time of his death summed up his long and eventful career in the following words:

> The deceased also served in various other parts of North America under his uncle, Colonel Schuyler, and after being promoted to the rank of Colonel, and commanding for many years the 8th Regiment, he retired to Dumfries, the native town of Mrs. De. Peyster, the faithful follower of his fortunes in every situation – in camp and in quarters – amidst savage tribes and polished communities – in the most distant stations of Upper Canada, as well as in walled and garrisoned cities. Indeed, we may here state, without the slightest qualification, that there never was a more venerable and tenderly attached pair. For more than fifty years, they shared the same bed, without having been separated in any one instance; and altogether the gallant old Colonel's bearing to his faithful and long-cherished spouse, resembled more what we ween of the age of chivalry, than the altered, and, as we suspect, not improved manners of the present times.

> In his person Colonel De Peyster was tall, soldierlike, and commanding; in his manners, easy, affable and open; in his affections, warm, generous, and sincere; in his principles, and particularly his political principles, firm even to inflexibility. No man, we believe, ever possessed more of the principle of vitality. Old age, which had silvered his hair, and furrowed his cheeks, appeared to make no impression on his inner man, and those who knew him best declare that, up to the period of his last illness, his mind appeared as active, and his intellect as vigorous as they were fifty years ago. When the weather permitted, he still took his accustomed exercise, and walked round the billiard table, or bestrode his gigantic charger, apparently with as little difficulty as a man of middle age. When so mounted, we have often fancied we beheld in him the last connecting link betwixt the old and new schools of military men.[18]

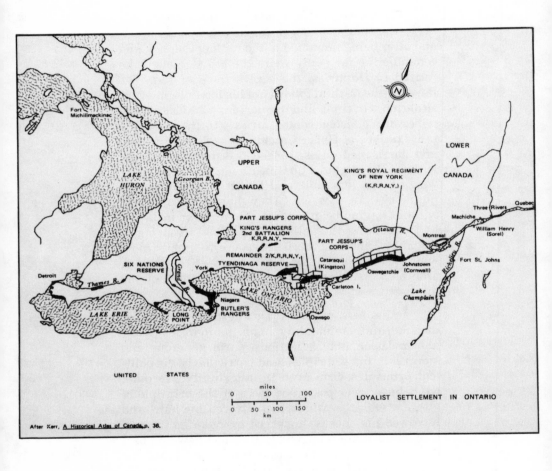

LOYALIST SETTLEMENT IN ONTARIO

After Kerr, A Historical Atlas of Canada, p. 36.

54

# Chapter Four

## Matthew Dolsen
## (c. 1750–1813)
## Tavern-keeper and Trader

*Among the Loyalists were a considerable number who were of Dutch origin, descendants of the early settlers of New Netherland. One of these was Matthew Dolsen, whose father had settled as a pioneer in the Susquehanna Valley of Pennsylvania. He, too, became a farmer there in Northumberland County, but in 1778 was forced to abandon his property and escape to Niagara.*

The first settlers of Dutch origin arrived in Detroit as early as the 1760s. By then, one branch of the Dolsen family of New York State had taken up residence in the fort of Detroit, which had recently been taken from the French by the British. The Dolsens were part of a large colonial family which had been founded in America more than 100 years earlier and had numerous members, with a branch in Pennsylvania as well as New York State. Not much is known about these early settlers of Detroit except that a son, Matthew Dolsen, was born there about 1770. This Matthew Dolsen (c. 1770-c. 1813), however, must be distinguished from the subject of this narrative, the better-known and somewhat older Matthew Dolsen (d. 1813), a Loyalist who fought with Butler's Rangers and opened a tavern and store in Detroit in 1781. Not only are the two names identical, but both men lived in the same area at more or less the same time, both leaving Detroit near the end of the eighteenth century to settle along the banks of the Thames. These men, however, did represent two different branches of the Dolsen family, which had originated in New York State where the family had settled after its immigrant ancestor's arrival from the Netherlands in the seventeenth century.

A *typical* *farmhouse,* *Dalfsen,* *the* *Netherlands* *where* *the*
*van* *Dalfsen* *family* *originally* *came* *from* *in* *the* *Province* *of*
*Overijssel.*

*This old farm building in Dalfsen is also typical of the province of Overijssel in the Netherlands.*

Both men spelled their name "Dolsen," but this was only one of many different forms of their surname which appeared in various records of the time. When their ancestor arrived from the Netherlands most settlers were known simply by their Christian names combined with that of their father. The Dolsen's ancestor was a ship-builder called Jan Gerritsen (Jan, son of Gerrit). However, within two or three generations after their arrival Dutch settlers selected surnames, often choosing to recall their town of origin in the Netherlands. Jan Gerritsen's descendants chose the name "van Dalfsen" (from Dalf-sen), since the family originally came from the village of Dalfsen or the surrounding area, in the Province of Overijssel in the eastern part of the Netherlands. As the number of Jan Gerritsen's descendants grew, the name was changed many times: germanized from van Dolsen and van Dalsen to Van Dolzen; anglicized to Dalston, Dolsen, and finally Dolson. By coincidence both Matthew Dolsens of Detroit used the same spelling of the name, although they represented different branches of the family, one coming, or so it is thought, from New York State, the other definitely from Pennsylvania.

Dutch country people such as the van Dalfsens had been in great demand in New Netherland during the days of its settlement in the seventeenth century. Although the chief interest of the West Indian Company was the fur trade, members of the five "chambers" or boards of trade which governed the company knew that settlers were essential. Only permanent settlement by good farmers like the van Dalfsens, who would make the soil productive, would give the colony lasting stability. Special shipments of sheep, horses, and cattle were brought in during the late 1620s. Then, in 1629, a policy was set up by which huge tracts of land were made into great manorial estates called "patroonships." If a responsible Dutch citizen would promise to settle 50 adult Dutch immigrants, he could obtain a grant of land stretching 26 kilometres along one bank of any navigable stream or 13 kilometres along both banks, and as far inland as he thought suitable.

However, tenants had come to the New World in search of land of their own. By the time Jan Gerritsen

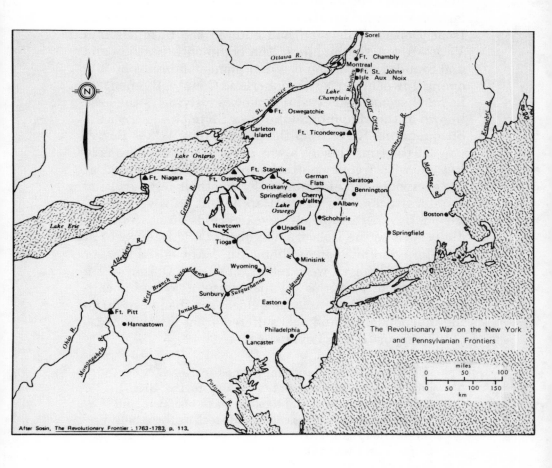

The Revolutionary War on the New York and Pennsylvanian Frontiers

miles
0    50    100
0   50   100   150
km

After Sosin, The Revolutionary Frontier, 1763-1783, p. 113.

59

[van Dalfsen] arrived in the middle of the seventeenth century, the West Indian company had been forced to allow farmers to obtain land without becoming tenants of some great *patroon*. Within the next century, Dutch farmers joined other immigrants, many of them German or English in origin, in opening up new frontiers along the Delaware and Susquehanna. One of these was a young farmer, a descendant of Jan Gerritsen [van Dalfsen] named Isaac Dolsen. This man had entered the Susquehanna Valley about the middle of the eighteenth century and had founded one of the original pioneer families of Wyoming Township in Northumberland County. By the 1770s he had become a successful landowner, living in the area known as the Manor of Sunbury, or Shamokin, across the Susquehanna River from the present-day Wilkes-Barre.

At the time this area was particularly dangerous to live in, with frequent attacks from Indians incensed at the encroachment of white settlers on their territory, and counterattacks by white settlers intent on revenge. Occasionally, there were unprovoked raids on peaceful Indians such as the Dolsen's neighbours, the Delawares at the Moravian mission at Shamokin. Many of the pioneer farmers of the area were rebels, but Isaac Dolsen was a strong supporter of the Loyalist cause, as were his children. Matthew Dolsen, Isaac's eldest son, had been farming independently and also suffered great losses because of his support of the Loyalist cause:

> [He was] harassed and imprisoned in Northumberland Jail on account of his loyalty to the British Government, and was obliged to leave his farm, and lost his crop and all his cattle and stock as the rebels threatened his life. He fled to York to join General Clinton and was taken and imprisoned and one of his brothers was killed by his side. . . . He made his escape after being long confined, and came in to Niagara, and since to this place [Detroit].[1]

With other Loyalists, Isaac Dolsen and his family escaped to Niagara in 1778, abandoning the family farm in the Manor of Sunbury, which was later confiscated. In the same group of Loyalist refugees as the Dolsens were the Fields, close neighbours in Pennsylvania and related by marriage.[2] In Niagara, Isaac and Matthew Dolsen and two of the three Field sons, Daniel and Nathan, joined Butler's Rangers, a Loyalist regiment under the command of Lieutenant Colonel John Butler. For three years they fought the rebels, in 1778 in their native Wyoming Valley, later in other territory. Then in 1781, Matthew Dolsen arrived in Detroit, perhaps in his capacity as a soldier with Butler's Rangers, for companies of this regiment were stationed in Detroit for some time. It is certain he was there as early as May 1781 for at that time he purchased a lot in the fort from Gregor McGregor and began to work as a trader and merchant. Eventually, he kept an inn there.

Meanwhile, Isaac Dolsen remained in the Niagara region with other members of his large family. He settled there as a farmer, together with many other soldiers of Butler's Rangers after the regiment had disbanded in June 1784. However, it appears that Isaac was greatly disappointed in the arrangements made for Loyalist farmers there and was one of the chief petitioners in a formal complaint about the situation. Eventually, he also moved to the Detroit River region where his son, Matthew, had already settled. On 2 September 1784 Isaac Dolsen bought a farm at Petite Côte on the east side of the Detroit River, paying £500 to the French farmer, Theophile Lemay, who had developed it. Isaac Dolsen thus became the first person of Dutch heritage to settle in the area known as Essex County. He was followed just a week later by his son-in-law, Daniel Field, who bought the adjoining lot. However, Field soon sold it to Matthew Dolsen who by then had a well-established inn and store in Detroit. Matthew Dolsen did not live on his Petite Côte farm, but visited it from time to time. In 1793 he took visiting Quakers who were staying at his inn in Detroit over by boat to see his farm.

Petite Côte was part of the area of planned settlement laid out by the French in 1749-1751, and populated during the next few years by families moving over from the Detroit side of the river. By the time the Dolsens bought lots there, it had been settled by the French for 30 years and was a most attractive prospect. A soldier,

James Smith, who was captured by the Indians and taken to Detroit when it was still in French control in 1758 has left a vivid description of Petite Côte:

> Opposite to Detroit, and below it, was originally a prairie, and laid off in lots of about sixty rods broad, and a great length: each lot is divided into two fields, which they cultivate year about. The principal grain that the French raised in these fields was spring wheat and peas. They built all their houses on the front of these lots on the river side; and as the banks of the river are very low, some of the houses are not above three or four feet above the surface of the water; yet they are in no danger of being disturbed by freshes, as the river seldom rises above eighteen inches.
> As dwelling-houses, barns, and stables are all built on the front of these lots; at a distance it appears like a continued row of houses in a town, on each side of the river for a long way. These villages, the town, the river and the plains, being all in view at once, affords a most delightful prospect.[3]

These French farms with their orchards of pears (the well-known "French" pear trees), apples, peaches, cherries, and plums, the stock brought, so it is said, from Normandy, would have changed very little in the 25 years that had passed between James Smith's description and 1784 when Isaac Dolsen bought his farm. As elsewhere in the province at the time, this land actually belonged to the Indians and Isaac Dolsen, like other settlers, was technically a squatter. This problem was not resolved until 1790 when most of the land which is now Essex County was bought from the Indians with trade goods.

Isaac Dolsen had at least one child added to his large family while they were living at Petite Côte, for a descendant stated that his grandfather was born at "Sandwich" in 1785.[4] Soon, however, Isaac left Petite Côte to become a squatter in the valley of the Lower Thames. A survey made by Patrick McNiff in the year 1790 shows the Isaac Dolsen farm on the south side, in what would become Raleigh Township. This is the farm where Dolsens live to this day.

By 1789 Matthew Dolsen, too, had an establishment on the Thames River in what is now Dover Township, across the river from the Isaac Dolsen farm. For some time after becoming a squatter on the Thames, he divided his time between managing his inn in Detroit where his family lived only occasionally, farming his lot at Petite Côte, and making frequent trips to his establishment and permanent home on the Thames. In 1792 he received the grant for his land on the Thames, which he had in the meantime improved. Yet he continued to live part of the year in Detroit, still being listed there in 1796 as a resident who wanted to remain under the British flag.

Although the Americans had won their independence in 1783, the British refused to abandon Detroit and other forts in the western region. This was in part an attempt to pressure the Americans into compensating Loyalists such as the Dolsens for their property losses. As much as ten years after the end of the war, English fur traders and Canadian settlers such as Matthew Dolsen still continued to carry out profitable fur trading in what was technically American territory. When Detroit finally passed officially to the Americans in 1796, the town became American in fact as well as name. Soon, Matthew Dolsen moved permanently to his estate on the Thames, where his descendants remained until the farm was sold in 1915.

While Matthew Dolsen was running an inn in Detroit, and later, from his farm on the Thames River, he was closely associated with the Moravian missionaries and their Indian converts mentioned in the previous chapter. Although in 1781 Major De Peyster had provided the destitute Moravians with food from the King's store in Detroit, and had written to Moravians in England for donations, this had not been sufficient. David Zeisberger, the Moravian missionary, turned to Matthew Dolsen for help. Although he knew that the newly-arrived inn-keeper was himself not in particularly good financial circumstances, having then just left service with Butler's Rangers, Zeisberger asked for assistance with the words:

> There are, we know, many wealthier gentlemen in
> this place than you are, who could help us if they

63

would, but perhaps they are not so worthy of doing
it. We ask that favour of you.[5]

Dolsen, a kind man, agreed.

From the fall of 1791 to the spring of 1792, the two
Dolsen children, Isaac and John, attended a short-lived
mission school set up by the Moravians at a place near
present-day Amherstburg. There, in 1791, the missionaries received assistance from two senior officers of the
Indian Department, Deputy Superintendent Alexander
McKee and Captain Matthew Elliott. They were allowed
to settle on McKee's plantation of 2,000 acres (800 hectares)
and to use Elliott's large house on his neighbouring land
downriver, while the Indian converts camped on the
grounds between. Soon a church was built and the settlement given a name: "Die Warte" or "The Watch Tower."

A number of records in David Zeisberger's diary show
the young Dolsen children were among those attending
the school, taught by Brother Gottlob Sensemann:

> Monday, Nov. 20 (1791) With some of our Indians,
> who came by water from Detroit, came also Mrs.
> Dolsen, to visit her two children, who are at
> school here with Br. Sensemann.[6]

> Monday, April 2 (1792) Samuel went to Detroit, and
> took there with him Dolsen's two children.[7]

John, 15, the older of the two, was born about 1776
in Fishing Creek, Pennsylvania, and was only two when
the family had escaped to Niagara. Isaac, the second son,
born in Detroit 23 August 1786, was only five when he
went to school at Die Warte.

The school attended by the two Dolsen boys was one
of the first in what is now Ontario. As in all Moravian
mission schools, music was an important subject. The
teacher, Brother Sensemann, also stressed the importance of penmanship, and it was said that his students
wrote a better English hand than the mercantile clerks
in Detroit. He had an unusual method of teaching which
had been developed by his fellow missionary, David Zeisberger. First he would write to his students, using the
Unami language. He then asked for answers to these

notes. These he would read aloud in class where the writer and his fellow students could hear his remarks, and all could benefit from his corrections. No doubt he adapted this method to teach the Dolsen boys, who were English-speaking. According to the Moravian records Brother Sensemann's students were greatly attached to him, for he was an entertaining teacher who made all school work seem interesting. He was also a practical man, a master of many trades which he taught to his pupils. It was an unusually fine opportunity for the Dolsen boys to attend this Moravian school, where they were welcomed as boarders although they were not members of the group, being Methodist in religion.

The friendly relations between the Dolsens and the Moravians are illustrated by an entry from Zeisberger's diary on an occasion when Mrs. Dolsen, coming from Lake Erie by ship on her way to Detroit, passed the mission where her two sons were boarders. "We sent aboard some refreshment[s] in the way of garden sauce and butter, which were very welcome."[8]

On Tuesday, 12 April 1792, the Moravians assembled for the last time in their chapel at Die Warte, and the school was closed in preparation for a move to the Thames and a new settlement they named Fairfield. The two Dolsen boys returned to their home in Detroit and eventually to the Dolsen farm on the Thames, not far downriver from the Moravians.

When the Dolsen family moved permanently to the lot on the Thames which Matthew had selected as the site of his home, there was much hard work to be done to develop the property, for when he had first come there a few years earlier as a trader there was no cleared area of land large enough upon which to build a barn. By the spring of 1792 the family had built a shelter and begun to improve the land on Lot 19 in what was to become Dover Township, at a narrows in the Thames River.

Other members of the large Dolsen family settled nearby as well. Isaac Dolsen Senior, who had led his family to Niagara as a Loyalist, had seven children: Isaac, Jacob, Matthew, Peter, Daniel, Hannah, and Betsey. He brought his large family to the Thames, where he settled in what is now Raleigh Township. He was quite elderly by the time the family cleared their land, and was unable to undertake much of the hard labour required to improve the property. However, his children were successful in establishing what was to become one of the finest farms in the vicinity. This passed from the elderly Loyalist Isaac to his son Daniel (1773-1853), then to Daniel's grandson, Gilbert H. Dolsen, and eventually was passed on from father to son through the generations to the present day. The owners of the family farm, now designated a Century Farm, are at present Roger and Winifred Dolsen.

The Matthew Dolsen farm on the other side of the Thames River developed in quite a different way, soon growing into a large business establishment. Once Matthew Dolsen had moved from Detroit to stay permanently on his estate on the Thames River, he made rapid progress. He became one of the most popular of the traders with the local Indians, visiting the Moravian mission at Fairfield frequently and usually staying several days at a time, especially in the fall when the crops had been gathered and the Indians were eager to barter. From Dolsen's carefully kept journal in which he noted the details of his trading expeditions, the reader of the present day can obtain a detailed picture of the trade goods which Dolsen obtained from the North West Company to barter with the Indians. With him he brought brightly coloured blankets and cloth coats, woollen stockings, hats, striped belts, and supplies of pipes, knives, rifles, buttons, and pins. The Moravian missionaries took great care to prevent whiskey from being brought into the mission, and despised those who sold it directly to the Indians on their trips outside the mission grounds. Dolsen, however, was not one of these, and remained a close friend of the Moravians. In exchange for his goods Matthew Dolsen received rolls of furs, corn, cattle, and finely made brooms, baskets, and bowls. He was particularly interested in obtaining furs, including those of raccoon, otter, fox, and beaver, all of which were in great demand on the market. In addition, the mission supplied large quantities of corn for export, since their carefully tended fields were able to produce far more than was needed for the mission.

Matthew Dolsen became greatly concerned about the annual distribution of gifts from the King to the Indians,

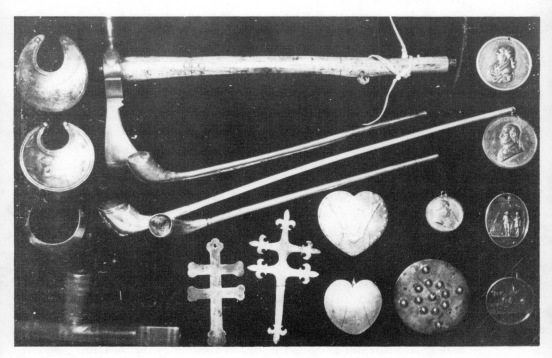

*Trade silver typical of that used in the trade with Indians, some of which was manufactured by silversmiths at Montreal, at Detroit and at the Loyalist settlement on Lake Erie near the Matthew Elliott estate.*

an event which took place each fall at Fort Malden, at Amherstburg when the Indian agent there, Alexander McKee, and later, Matthew Elliott, gave generous gifts to the Indians from the large warehouse that Elliott kept on his property there. Each year at a formal ceremony the King's gifts were distributed near the warehouse where, on a lawn, a stake had been placed for each tribe in the area, and near it the gifts had been piled. These valuable gifts included practical items such as blankets and clothing. However, the occasion also gave the Indian messengers, sent to Malden to represent the tribe and receive the King's gifts, an opportunity to obtain liquor. The mission Indians were unable to resist this temptation and returned year after year empty-handed, in a sorry state, having traded the King's gifts for liquor. This situation distressed not only the Moravian missionaries but also Matthew Dolsen, who employed the Indians on his busy estate. He was unhappy about the annual difficulties with his workmen due to the distribution of the gifts. Eventually, he wrote to the authorities asking that the Moravian Indians be given their gifts in another way, either having them sent to the mission or allowing a missionary or trusted messenger to go to the ceremony in their stead. This request was not granted. Instead, to the consternation of Matthew Dolsen and the missionaries, the reply was that Christian Indians who would not defend the King in times of war (for the Moravians were pacifists who remained neutral in wartime) would no longer be issued the annual gifts. This blow was softened by the fact that sympathetic Indian agents at Malden quietly continued to give annual gifts to the Christian Indians, delivering them for some years to the mission at Fairfield.

The Matthew Dolsen Thames settlement continued to grow into an impressive estate. Soon it included a gristmill, distillery, tavern, and blacksmith's shop. Ships were even built there, including an 80-ton pine-timbered boat for the North West Company, to be used in the fur trade.

Matthew Dolsen's estate became known simply as "Dolsen's," and continued to grow in importance. It became the centre of commercial activities on the Thames and remained so for many years. As such it played a role in the War of 1812, when the growing hostility between

*Mounted American forces charging British troops and Indians during the battle which took place not at Dolsen's Farm, which had earlier been Procter's intention, but rather about five kilometres from Moraviantown.*

the United States and Canada led to an American invasion of Canada. On Sunday, 12 July 1812 the Moravian missionary, Brother Dencke, arrived at Dolsen's to conduct the usual church service in the barn to find that only elderly men, such as Matthew Dolsen himself, women, and children were present, since all men of military age had left for camp at Sandwich. There, at Dolsen's that Sunday, they were unaware that that very day General Hull and an American army of 2,500 men had invaded Canada above abandoned Sandwich.

Soon post riders rode three or four times a week from Niagara to Malden, travelling this distance at the breakneck pace of two and a half days to cover the entire route, following rough forest trails. These riders had to change their horses every ten or fifteen miles. When they reached the Thames they were given fresh mounts of ponies from the Indian mission and supplies from Dolsen's. The Thames was patrolled by Indians from Fairfield "on the request of Mr. Dolsen, Sr., so that the inhabitants would at once be notified if anyone inimically minded were to show himself here."[9]

Within three days of the landing at Sandwich, General Hull and 200 troops reached Dolsen's on their way up the Thames towards the Indian mission at Fairfield. Their stated intention was to provide protection to those who remained neutral and show no quarter to those who opposed them. American agents were active in the area, gauging the strength of defence and testing the loyalty of those who had already deserted the militia and taken to the fields. The Indians had left Fairfield and hidden their valuables in the woods.

But in spite of the influx of American and British troops and spies into the area, and the general threatening unrest, Matthew Dolsen was spared any involvement in actual warfare. This broke out 15 months after Hull's invasion of Canada, when on 5 October 1813 American troops under General William Harrison attacked Fairfield and fought the Battle of the Thames. Six weeks earlier, however, Matthew Dolsen had died. On 19 August 1813 "Indians and Whites, Protestants and Catholics," some of whom had travelled from many miles away, gathered at Dolsen's to attend his funeral. Two clergymen were

*Winnifred Dolson, widow of the late Roger Dolson, and her son Allen, display family heirlooms found in the storerooms of their farm on the Raleigh River Road, founded by Isaac Dolsen in 1783.*

present. The Moravian missionary, Brother Dencke, conducted the funeral service in honour of Matthew Dolsen's kindness as the protector of the Indian mission. The Methodist minister, the circuit-rider Ninian Holmes, rose at the end of the service and affirmed the words spoken in eulogy of Matthew Dolsen by Brother Dencke. Dolsen was buried in the wood behind the family home.

On 15 October 1813, only a week after the Battle of the Thames, Matthew Dolsen's estate was settled. John Dolsen, the eldest son, by now a man of 37, inherited Lot 19 in Dover Township and the tavern, while Isaac, by then 27 years of age, received lot 18 and several other properties in the area. For many years, these farms on the Thames were managed by members of the Dolsen family who inherited them generation after generation, but eventually they were sold outside the family. Dolsen's as a manufacturing and trading centre, was eventually eclipsed by Chatham, which began to grow rapidly in the 1820s and 1830s.

Before leaving the Dolsen family, mention must be made of the "other Matthew Dolsen," who was born in Detroit about 1770 and died about 1813, shortly after the Battle of the Thames in which he took part. During the American Revolution, this Matthew Dolsen was a strong supporter of the rebel cause. Nevertheless he settled on the Thames River about the same time as his namesake, raising a family of five children together with his wife, Elizabeth Willits of Detroit, formerly of Pennsylvania.

When the War of 1812 broke out he was pressed into service with the British Army and taken from the Thames to Sandwich. There he deserted and escaped to Detroit where he joined Hull's army. When General Hull surrendered Detroit to a British, Canadian and Indian force in August 1812, Dolsen scaled the pickets of the fort and fled to Chillicothe, Ohio. There, because of his knowledge of the Thames River area, he became an asset to the Americans when they invaded in 1813. He acted as a guide for the invaders and was present at the Battle of Moraviantown, when the mission was burned to the ground. Meanwhile, Dolsen's wife and five young children, all under eight years of age, moved from the Thames to Detroit on 20 October 1813. There the family moved in

*Although many of the caskets from the original Dolson Cemetery have fallen into the Thames River and been lost through the effects of erosion, the recovered tombstones have been placed in cement foundations in a row along the river by Raleigh Township and the Lower Thames Valley Conservation Authority.*

with the Willits and this branch on the Dolsen family remained in Detroit, where its members have been active in business circles for the past century.

The two Matthew Dolsens, were similar in name, background, age and eventual place of settlement – Detroit and the valley of the Lower Thames – yet they chose differing loyalties: the one a traitor to his neighbours, the other a defender.

Encampment at Dolsen's Farm on 4 October 1813, *by J.C.H.*
*Forster, dated 1965. After Brigadier General Henry Proctor*
*abandoned Detroit, and then Sandwich, he moved his men on*
*to Dolsen's. At this settlement established 25 years earlier by the*
*Loyalist Matthew Dolsen, they paused briefly before going on to*
*Moraviantown where they fought the Battle of the Thames.*

*A man dressed up as a "devil" visiting a Mandingo town,
according to a description by the early explorers Richard Job-
son and Mungo Park: a scene certainly familiar to the Loyalist
Richard Pierpoint from his youth in Bondu.*

# Chapter Five

# Richard Pierpoint
# (c. 1745–c. 1838)
# Black Loyalist

*Brought to America as a slave at the age of 16, Richard Pierpoint spent his youth in servitude. In 1780 he arrived in Niagara where he joined Butler's Rangers. For three years, together with Matthew Dolsen and other Rangers he engaged in commando-type forays into American territory. At the end of the American Revolution he settled, as did some of the other Rangers, in the Niagara Peninsula. Later, he fought once again in the War of 1812, defending Canada against American invasion. During his long life – for he lived to be over 90 – he treasured his early memories of his native land of Bondu, a small kingdom in the interior of West Africa.*

Richard Pierpoint was born in about 1745 in the kingdom of Bondu, a small country now part of Senegal but then a separate Moslem state. It can be described as an elevated plateau, with hills in the central and southern parts. The higher land is unproductive, and is covered with stunted trees, but the lower country is extremely fertile. The trees which grow there luxuriantly in their natural state include valuable fruit trees, particularly beautiful when in flower. There is a dry and rainy season, and during the latter the streams which criss-cross the country fill with water and become rushing torrents bringing fresh new growth to the valleys. The climate is moderate and pleasant, and crops grow well.

In the eighteenth century most of the villages of Bondu were situated along the Faleme, an important branch of the Senegal River. When the Scottish explorer Mungo Park visited it in 1795 he remarked on its fine civilization, which reminded him of North Africa. While there was no dense forest, there were groves of tall acacia

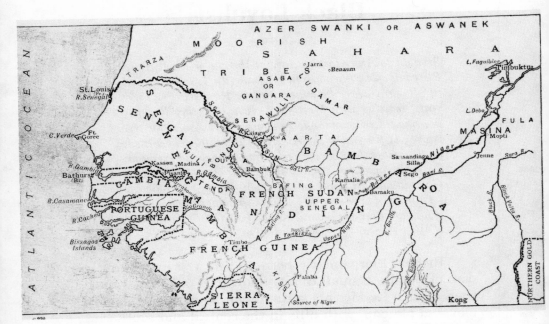

*Map of the Senegambia region showing the location of Bondu,
the homeland of the black Loyalist Richard Pierpoint.*

trees. The women dressed in fine gauze clothes, and wore beads and pieces of amber as jewellry. Large troops of donkeys rather than human labour, transported merchants' goods across the country. Many of the loads were of elephant tusks, because elephants were still to be found in great numbers in the mountainous areas, and the young men of Bondu were bold hunters. This ivory was intended for trade with the Arabs of the desert to the northeast, or with the traders in the advance posts of the French merchants on the upper Senegal River. As well as this ivory, corn, fish, and other food were prepared for sale. Also, Bondu lay directly on the ancient trade route by which the gold of Bambuk was transported to the European trading posts of the Gambia, the same trade route which was used to transport slaves from the Sudan down to the sea.

Bondu was ruled by Maka-Guiba (1728-1764), the Elimane (religious leader) of the country at the time of Richard Pierpoint's birth. The king was a member of a long dynasty of powerful rulers, one of whom, Malick Sy, was considered to be the founder of Bondu. According to tradition, Malick Sy was a Moslem who had made the pilgrimage to Mecca and had eventually, at the beginning of the seventeenth century, settled in Bondu, then practically an unpopulated wilderness. He and his successors made Bondu a sanctuary for refugees from all over the west of Africa, so that it grew steadily in population and political power, at the expense of its neighbours, the Malinke of Bambuk, who were forced to migrate elsewhere. There were frequent wars between the men of Bondu and the neighbouring states.

While Bondu was a Moslem state, not all of its people were Moslems, although many had been converted from their former religion, animism. When Richard Pierpoint was born almost one-half of the inhabitants were still animists. However, there were frequent new conversions due to the great tolerance of the Moslem leaders of the time, and also to the fine Koranic schools which they established in the villages. During Richard Pierpoint's lifetime, most of the people of Bondu became Moslems, including its officials and influential families. There is no evidence however that Richard Pierpoint was a Mos-

*The Fulas, who were the most powerful group in the mixed population of mid-eighteenth century Bondu, raised long-horned cattle. They were strikingly different from the Mandingos, who were farmers.*

lem. He was not able to write his name later in life when he was in Canada so it is unlikely that he attended school in Bondu as a child.

It is possible to conjecture that he belonged to the Mandingo tribe of Bondu, which together with the Fula, then made up the greatest part of the population. The Fula were the rulers of the country, descendants of nomadic cattle-raisers of mysterious origin who had lived side by side with the Mandingo farmers for many years and gradually, over many centuries, had migrated into many parts of western Africa, bringing with them the Moslem religion. They are now thought to have been partly of Berber and partly of Equatorial African origin. They considered themselves a white people, seemingly looking down on the Mandingos and other Blacks about them as if they were inferior. They were also contemptuous of Europeans. It is, then, unlikely that Richard Pierpoint, who was closely associated with his fellow Blacks during his career as a soldier and farmer in Canada, was a member of the semi-nomadic, cattle-raising Fula tribe. It is much more likely that he was a Mandingo, a tall, handsome tribe of dark-skinned Blacks, farmers who were close to the soil as well as being active hunters and traders.

The Mandingo people, too, were of uncertain origin, having come originally from the east. Some had intermarried with Arabs who came south into their great Mande empire, which stretched between the Upper Niger, the Gambia, and the Senegal. They were among the first black converts to the Moslem religion in the history of West Africa, and became a strong, warlike, and adventurous people over the centuries. When Richard Pierpoint was born, the Mandingo people were divided into two groups, the Bushrin who were Moslems and teetotallers, and the Kafir who were animists and fond of drinking native beer or wine. The subjugated Mandingo people were either freemen or slaves. Slaves were usually well treated and had many established rights, and under the ownership of a good chieftain, were allowed to live peaceably unless they committed a crime. If they did so, they were sold by their masters, either north to the Sahara, where a slave trade had been carried on for centuries, or to dealers who delivered them to European slave traders down river, for

81

*Elephants wreaked considerable destruction upon the small palmtrees and other vegetation of Bondu in their search for fresh leaves and fruit.*

transport to America. The Mandingos were friendly in their contacts with British explorers and traders in the nineteenth century. They were an exuberant people, fond of dancing and music, and much attached to the sport of wrestling. They were loyal to their king, Maka-Guiba, although he was a Fula ruler, in sole command of the entire country, able to make war or peace as he wished. In Richard Pierpoint's youth, the country was frequently at war.

When Richard Pierpoint was a young teenager, his king went to war against a neighbouring ruler, the King of Fouta. This powerful king, jealous of the great prosperity enjoyed by the people of Bondu, sent an inflammatory letter daring Maka-Guiba to fight to the death. The people of Bondu won the war, which was followed immediately by another one, fought by their king against one of his traditional enemies, the chief of Farabanna. But this time the men of Bondu lost. Maka-Guiba was killed, and many of his warriors were killed or captured in the general disarray which followed the final battle.

Some 60 years later, Richard Pierpoint mentioned that he "was made a prisoner" about 1760. It could well be that this event occurred in this same war, for this was the greatest defeat of the Bondu warriors in his time, and occurred about the year 1764. In any case, he was taken prisoner about this time, when he was 16 years of age.

It is also possible that he was captured by an African slave hunter, for there were tribesmen who lived from the profits they could make by raiding enemy territory deliberately looking for victims to sell on the slave market. The white traders did not capture slaves themselves, for the African interior was far too dangerous to their health. They stayed at the coastline, where they had built trading stations at which they bought slaves from the African dealers.

After his sale to a native trader, possibly a Mandingo, for most trade was in the hands of members of this widespread tribe, including the area of the Senegal and Gambia Rivers right down to the Niger, Richard Pierpoint would have been taken downriver to the coast. There, trading stations and forts had been built by the British and the French. The British fort was called James Fort

*Usually prisoners of war or captives of slave raiders, slaves such as Richard Pierpoint were forced to march to the trading stations on the coast.*

and was the main British settlement on the Gambia River. The French had built two forts on the coast of Senegal, but the British claimed exclusive rights to trade on the Gambia "for the encouragement of plantations in America."[1]

How slaves such as Richard Pierpoint were brought to market at James Fort has been described in detail by Francis Moore, a factor and writer for the Royal Africa Company from 1730-1735:

> The same merchants bring down elephants' teeth, and in some years slaves to the amount of two thousand, most of which they say are prisoners taken in war. They buy them from the different princes who take them; many of them are Bumbrongs and Petcharies, nations who each of them have a different language, and are brought from a vast way inland.
>
> Their way of bringing them is, tying them by the neck with leather thongs, at about a yard distant from each other, thirty or forty in a string, having generally a bundle of corn, or an elephant's tooth upon each of their heads. On their way from the mountains they travel through very great woods, where they cannot for some days get water, so they carry in skin-bags enough to support them for that time.
>
> Besides the slaves that the merchants bring down, there are many brought along the river. These are taken in war as the former are, or else men condemned for crimes, or else people stolen, which is very frequent. The company's servants never buy any of the last, if they suspect it, without sending for the Alcade, or chief men of the place, and consulting with them about the matter. Since this slave trade has been used, all punishments are changed into slavery; there being an advantage on such condemnations, they strain for crimes very hard in order to get the benefit of selling the criminal. Not only murder, theft and adultery are punished by selling the criminal for a slave, but every trifling crime is punished in the same manner.

At the trading station Richard Pierpoint was held with other slaves until he was sold to a white dealer, and branded before being put aboard a slave ship and taken to America.

Waiting for Richard Pierpoint and his fellow slaves at the coast were dealers who imprisoned them with other groups of slaves until merchants, in this case from the Royal African Company, arrived to buy them and take them to America. While they were in captivity awaiting purchase and shipment they were often cruelly treated. Moore writes:

> About midnight our ensign was called down by the sentinels, who were on duty, in order to prevent the slaves from making their escape, they having got an iron bar out of the slave house window; but it was then too small for a man to get out at, so they were taken and secured in another place for that night, and on the next day the ringleader of them being found out, and proving to be an old offender, he was ordered one hundred lashes.[2]

Slaves were considered a commodity, and formed the most important "export product" of the Gambia region at this time, with about 2,000 slaves being shipped to American destinations each year. Among them were some Fula and Mandingos, but they were not considered to be the most desirable slaves for heavy work on southern sugar plantations, as they were not believed to be the most industrious farmers. They were thought to serve best as personal servants. That was to be the fate of Richard Pierpoint, for he was bought by the Royal African Company representatives at the coast, and sent by ship to the Middle Colonies (perhaps New York), where he was bought by a British officer to serve as his personal servant.

In 1780, after serving 20 years as a slave, Richard Pierpoint made his way through the wilderness of upper New York State to Niagara. The British had offered freedom to all who would desert their masters and fight on the Loyalist side in the American Revolution. Pierpoint joined Butler's Rangers in Niagara where Mohawks from the Mohawk Valley of New York and pioneer farmers, many of them of Dutch or Palatinate German origin, were among those engaged in a guerrilla warfare against the Americans in upper New York State and Western Pennsylvania. There were other Blacks who fought with him

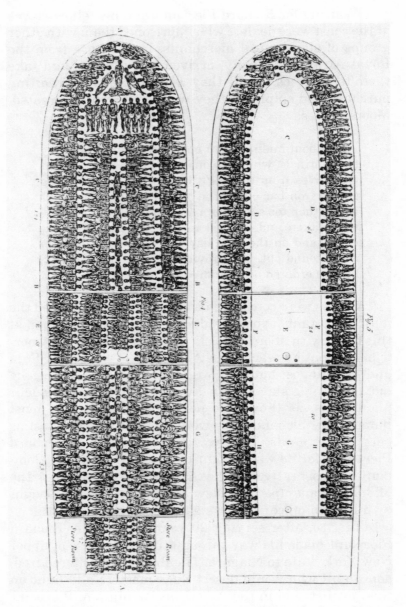

*A detail from a plan of the slave ship* Brookes *which carried 454 slaves in indescribably crowded and unhealthy conditions; the rule rather than the exception. Only strong and healthy slaves such as Pierpoint survived the ordeal.*

in the ranks of Butler's Rangers, other slaves who had travelled to Niagara to find freedom.

Richard Pierpoint's name appears on a list drawn up for General Haldimand of the Loyalists who submitted their names for Crown lands located opposite Fort Niagara. From this it may be seen that he was then in the Niagara area, and wanted to settle there. Apparently he did so, for according to the Grantham Township Papers, Richard Pierpoint was granted Lots 13 and 14 in Concession 6 on 18 January 1791. He sold these two lots in 1804. He also appears to have owned at one time or another still other lots in the area of present-day St. Catharines, however, it is difficult to trace these in the early land records. Pierpoint's will shows that he thought he owned Lot 13 in Concession 8 of Grantham Township, but the land records do not indicate that this lot was ever registered in his name. According to all the evidence, after 1784 he spent most, of not all, of his days in Grantham Township, where his name became associated with a local landmark, "Dick's Creek."[3]

Already at this early time, when Upper Canada was established in 1791, the institution of slavery was being challenged and fought in areas under British rule. That year, William Wilberforce introduced a bill in the House of Commons in London in an attempt to stop traders from bringing slaves into British colonies. He was supported in his work by another reformer, Colonel John Graves Simcoe, who had fought as a British officer in the American Revolutionary War. Simcoe became the first Lieutenant-governor of Upper Canada. When he arrived in Niagara, the capital of Upper Canada under the new name of Newark, he found that the institution of slavery was accepted, and that many of the officers and leaders of Upper Canada owned slaves and did not question the justice of this practice. In 1793 his efforts to correct this situation resulted in a new act being passed, one which confirmed the status of slaves who had already been brought into Upper Canada, requiring their owners to feed and clothe them in a suitable manner. No longer could more slaves be brought into the country. Also, any child born in Upper Canada of a slave mother would gain freedom at the age of 25. This new law began to change

To His Excellency John Graves Simcoe Esq.r &c.a Governor Upper Canada, Colonel Commanding the Forces in said Province &c. &c. &c.

The Petition of the Free Negroes.

Humbly Sheweth

That there are a number of Negroes in this part of the Country many of whom have been Soldiers during the late war between Great Britain & America, and others who were born free with a few who have come into Canada since the Peace,— your Petitioners are desirous of settling adjacent to each other in order that they may be enabled to give assistance (in work) to those amongst them who may most want it, Your Petitioners therefore humbly Pray, that their situation may be taken into consideration, and if your Excellency should see fit to allow them a Tract of Country to settle on, separate from the white settlers, your Petitioners hope their behaviour will be such as to shew, that Negroes are capable of being industrious, and that in loyalty to the Crown they are not deficient.

And Your Memorialist Will as in duty Bound Ever Pray.

*Richard Pierpoint was one of the blacks who signed the Petition of the Free Negroes addressed to Colonel John Graves Simcoe, asking for permission to found an all-black settlement for mutual support under the trying conditions of pioneer life.*

public opinion about slavery. Soon an anti-slavery reform movement gained strength and slavery declined. More and more slaves were set free by their masters. By the time the British Parliament passed a law to abolish slavery throughout the British Empire in 1834, when Richard Pierpoint was in his 80s, slavery no longer existed in Upper Canada, having died out many years earlier.

During the earliest period when Pierpoint was living in Niagara, he was one of the minority of Blacks who was a free man. In 1805 when Michigan was declared to be a territory, it was decreed that slavery would not be permitted there. Some of the Indian agent Matthew Elliott's slaves escaped across the Detroit River to Detroit, where they were organized as a black militia and where they drilled in preparation to rescue other black slaves from the Canadian side of the river. Nonetheless, some of these black militiamen deserted and returned to Canada where they settled in Amherstburg, near Fort Malden, forming a small black community there.

The threat of attack from the American side of the Detroit River continued to loom. After years of concern about imminent attack, on 12 July American troops invaded Canada near Sandwich, in the opening attack of the War of 1812. The Blacks of Amherstburg and of other parts of Upper Canada were greatly afraid that an American victory would send them back into slavery once again.

At this point, during the summer of 1812 shortly after the American invasion, the veteran Butler's Ranger, Richard Pierpoint, sent a petition to the British Army headquarters. Pierpoint requested that a special black company be mustered, bringing into Niagara Blacks from all parts of Upper Canada so that they might stand together and fight for their freedom. The petition was answered favourably, and within three months a special force was raised, made up of Blacks who came to Niagara from various parts of the province and gathered at the frontier to offer their services. They were put under the command of Captain Robert Runchey Senior, a white man, and were given the name "Captain Runchey's Company of Coloured Men." Later James Robertson, who is believed to have been black, and who had been a lieutenant in the Provincial Artificers, attached to the Army Engineers, took over the command. Richard Pierpoint, in accordance with the plan which he himself had suggested, joined this company to defend Canada.

During the War of 1812 Captain Runchey's Company of Coloured Men took part in many engagements. Early in 1813 they were part of the small force that defended the town of Niagara and Fort George against great odds, under a combined attack by the American army and navy. Under cover of the guns of the American battleships, the enemy soldiers attacked on two fronts, landing on the shore of Lake Ontario.[4]

Eventually forced to retreat, the defenders of Fort George suffered heavy losses, but it is not known how many of Captain Runchey's black volunteers were killed or wounded. Richard Pierpoint was not among these casualties and continued in service. Members of Runchey's Company continued to distinguish themselves in some of the major battles of the war, fighting at Queenston Heights, Stoney Creek, Lundy's Lane, and in many smaller engagements with the enemy. Under General Roger Sheaffe, at Queenston Heights, they fought side by side with the Mohawk Indians of Brantford, under the leadership of John Brant, the 18-year-old son of the late Joseph Brant.

Captain Runchey's company fought gallantly for two years. In June 1814 the company was at Fort George, and a month later at Fort Mississauga, staying as a garrison when the main body of regular soldiers fell back to Twenty Mile Creek. By the end of the war the corps had become a labour force attached to the Department of the Quartermaster General and under the command of Captain George Fowler.

When the Coloured Company was disbanded at the close of the War of 1812, Richard Pierpoint remained in the Niagara Peninsula area. There he spent the remaining 24 years of his life, close to Fort Niagara which had been his headquarters when he had first arrived in Canada in 1780. At the close of the war, he first took up residence within the town of Niagara itself. There was a growing community of Blacks in this area close to the American border. Not only were there a number of former military men, but there were also recent arrivals of slaves from the United States. During the War of 1812 American

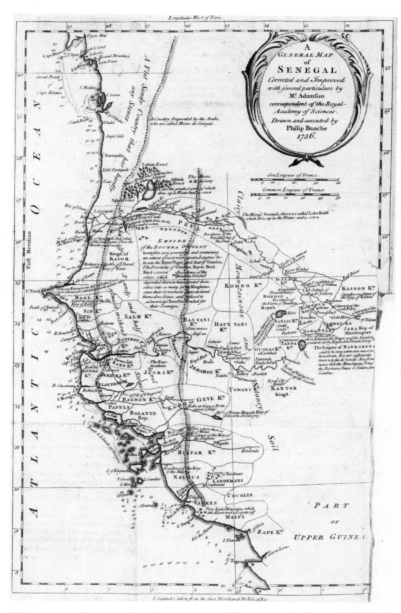

This general map of Senegal dating from the mid-1750s shows a path leading from the Senegal River to Bondu which may well be the route which Richard Pierpoint intended to follow in his return to Bondu if his petition to be returned to Africa had been successful.

soldiers had heard of the favourable laws, affecting Blacks and the anti-slavery movement in Canada and these rumours had been spread throughout the United States. Slaves in the United States began to escape across the border in ever-growing numbers, forming small communities along the border at Niagara, especially near St. Catharines.

Seven years after the close of the War of 1812, Richard Pierpoint became thoroughly discouraged with the conditions of his life. He had fallen into poverty, and was alone and without relatives in Upper Canada. Although he was now about 75 years old, he decided to once again send a petition to the government, but this time his plan was to ask to be sent back to Bondu to spend his remaining years with his own people.[5] On 21 July 1821 he sent the following petition to the authorities:

The Petition of Richard Pierpoint, now of the Town of Niagara, a Man of Colour, a native of Africa, and an inhabitant of this Province since the year 1780.

Most humbly showeth,

That Your Excellency's Petitioner is a native of Bondu in Africa; that at the age of Sixteen Years he was made a Prisoner and sold as a Slave; that he was conveyed to America about the year 1760, and sold to a British officer; that he served his Majesty during the American Revolutionary War in the Corps called Butler's Rangers; and again during the late American War in a Corps of Colour raised on the Niagara Frontier.

That Your Excellency's Petitioner is now old and without property; that he finds it difficult to obtain a livelihood by his labour; that he is above all things desirous to return to his native Country; that His Majesty's Government be graciously pleased to grant him any relief, he wishes it may be by affording him the means to proceed to England and from thence to a Settlement near the Gambia or Senegal Rivers, from Whence he could return to Bondu . . .

York Upper Canada
21st July 1821

94

Accompanying Richard Pierpoint's petition was a recommendation written by the Adjutant General of the Militia of Upper Canada, N. Coffin. He attested to Pierpoint's good character and fine service record in the following statements:

> I do hereby certify that Richard Pierpoint, a man of colour, served His Majesty, in North America, during the American Revolutionary War, in the Provincial Corps called Butler's Rangers.

> I further certify that the said Richard Pierpoint, better known by the name of Captain Dick, was the first colored man who proposed to raise a Corps of Men of Color on the Niagara Frontier, in the last American War; that he served in the said corps during that War, and that he is a faithful and deserving old Negro.[6]

While the petition is on file at the Public Archives of Canada, there is no record of an answer having been sent. If so, it was a negative one, for Richard Pierpoint continued to live in the Niagara Peninsula. However, the following year he received a grant of land as an acknowledgement of the role he had played in military service in the War of 1812. Several of the Blacks who had served in Captain Runchey's company received these grants of land in districts of Upper Canada newly opened for settlement. There were no obligations attached to these grants, so that the land could be occupied and improved, or sold to another settler. It was a free gift of land. Richard Pierpoint's grant was for 100 acres (40 hectares), one-half Lot 6, in the first concession of Garafraxa Township in Wellington County. This was then a wilderness which had just been surveyed. The first settlers had yet to arrive there. It is quite understandable that Pierpoint accepted the grant but, at his advanced age, did not consider moving into the wilderness to undertake the back-breaking work of a pioneer. Instead, he continued to live near Niagara, in Grantham Township where he now owned Lot 13 on the eighth concession, a site close to the important new waterway, the Welland Canal, built between 1824 and 1829. Although there is no record of the trans-

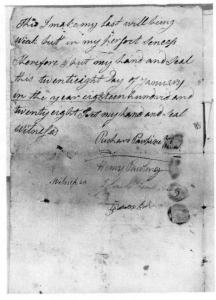

*A will written for Richard Pierpoint when he was over eighty years of age. It is signed with his mark, and witnessed by two well-known pioneers of St. Catharines, both of whom were active in local military history.*

action, he seems to have obtained the lot in Grantham Township granted to him about the same time, in any case after he wrote the petition in 1821 stating that he was living in poverty and without property.

No doubt Richard Pierpoint was disappointed that he had received no answer, or a negative one, to his petition asking to be sent back to Bondu. However, it appears that to have returned there would have been disastrous. The kingdom of Bondu lay in ruins, having been over-run in 1817 and 1818 by neighbouring enemies. It was no longer the beautiful, civilized, and prosperous country which he remembered from his youth. However, there was little contact between Bondu and other parts of the world at this time and it is unlikely that Richard Pierpoint heard of the ruin of his country.

Little is known of his last years except what is revealed by his will. On 28 January 1828 he prepared his last will and testament in the presence of a prominent local farmer, Henry Pawling, and two witnesses, John and Peter Tenbroeck. This will, signed with his mark, reads:

This is my last Will and Testament
in the Name of God Amen
I have no heirs nor relations. I make Lemuel Brown my heir and Executor. I do give to Lemuel Brown the one half of Lot Number Six in the first Concession of Garafraxa containing one hundred acres, to him, his heirs, administrators, and assigns forever. I likewise give Lemuel Brown Lot No. Thirteen in the eighth Concession of Grantham in the District of Niagara, to him, his heirs, and administrators, and assigns forever. I likewise do give Lemuel Brown, his heirs and assigns all my real and personal property, to him, his heirs, and assigns, and administrators forever, to make use of as he thinks proper. This I make my last will, being weak but in my perfect senses. Therefore I put my hand and seal this twenty-eighth day of January in the year eighteen hundred and twenty eight. I set my hand and seal:

Richard Pawpine (his mark)
Henry Pawling
witnesses: John R. Tenbroeck
Peter Tenbroeck[7]

Pierpoint's name was written "Pawpine" in this and other legal documents concerned with his estate. Yet the description of the lot in Garafraxa identifies Richard Pawpine as indeed Richard Pierpoint, who was granted the last half of Lot 6 in the first Concession of Garafraxa on 30 July 1822. The pronunciation of Pierpoint as "Pawpine" provides us with an echo from the past of this black warrior's soft African accent.

The last ten years of Richard Pierpoint's life were spent in Grantham Township, where he died about ten years after writing his will, at the age of about 90. On 28 September 1838 his heir, Lemuel Brown, a farmer in the Gore District of Halton County, claimed the estate of "Richard Pawpine, yeoman, deceased." No doubt Lemuel Brown had cared for his well-being during the last decade of his life. Brown's reward was the ownership of a lot in Wellington County in an area known to settlers wanting to farm as the "Queen's Bush."

His final years as a "yeoman and landowner" in Upper Canada, with a valuable legacy to leave to his friend Lemuel Brown, are a tribute to the enterprise of Richard Pierpoint, a warrior of Bondu who fought bravely for his new country, one which a fellow Black called "the best poor-man's country I know."

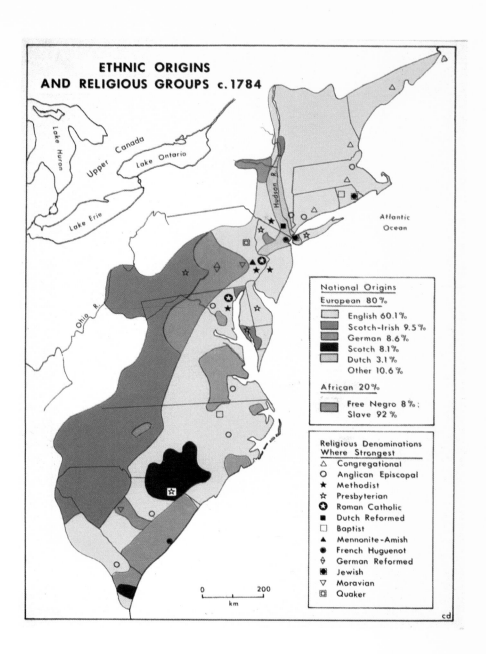

ETHNIC ORIGINS AND RELIGIOUS GROUPS c.1784

Lake Huron

Upper Canada

Lake Ontario

Lake Erie

Hudson R.

Atlantic Ocean

Ohio R.

**National Origins**

European 80%

English 60.1%
Scotch-Irish 9.5%
German 8.6%
Scotch 8.1%
Dutch 3.1%
Other 10.6%

African 20%

Free Negro 8%:
Slave 92%

**Religious Denominations Where Strongest**

△ Congregational
○ Anglican Episcopal
★ Methodist
☆ Presbyterian
✪ Roman Catholic
■ Dutch Reformed
□ Baptist
▲ Mennonite-Amish
◉ French Huguenot
⬧ German Reformed
⬛ Jewish
▽ Moravian
⊡ Quaker

0        200
km

cd

*A view of the Valley of the Guerbe River from Riggisberg, Switz-erland, the birthplace of Peter Etter, a Loyalist of Swiss origin.*

# Chapter Six

## Peter Etter
## (1715–1794)
## A Loyalist of Swiss Origin

*When the British evacuated Boston in March 1776, among the Loyalist refugees who were taken to Halifax by ship, along with the British Army, was Peter Etter. He had been born in Switzerland, but at the age of 22 had followed his father to America. After spending several years in Philadelphia and Boston, he settled permanently in Braintree (now Quincy), Massachusetts, where he was a stocking weaver. Forced to flee for their lives, Peter Etter and his family took refuge in Boston early in 1775. A year later, they left for Halifax where the seven surviving members of the family settled temporarily. While Peter and the younger of his children stayed on in Halifax, the older children founded branches of the Etter family in Westmorland and Chester. In later years, descendents of Peter Etter moved to Ontario and other parts of Canada where members of this widespread family of Swiss origin are to be found today.*

The Etter family of Switzerland is an ancient one, with roots in several cantons of the German-language areas of the country, including Freiburg and Bern. In the border region of these two cantons, one particular branch of the Etters lived, in an area stretching over the cantonal border and included members of the family in the parishes of Ferenbalm in Bern, and Kerzers and Murten in Freiburg. Local records show that the family to which Peter Etter could trace his roots was already to be found in Ferenbalm in 1462. A century later they were living in Kerzers, and it was there that Johannes Etter, the first member of the family to leave for America, was born in 1680.

At this time in history the Swiss were in a fortunate position. While the rest of Europe was involved in a

101

*View of the parish church of Thurnen, recently renovated to reveal its original medieval structure.*

succession of devastating wars, Switzerland was able to enjoy a long period of peace. In the average year sufficient wheat was grown in the western plain to supply the needs of people. However, in the eighteenth century economic conditions began to change for the worse, particularly in certain areas, such as the mountain regions of Bern.

Sometime between 1708 and 1712 Johannes Etter married Anna Sigrist of the neighbouring community of Ried and moved across the cantonal border into Bern, settling in the small community of Riggisberg overlooking the Lake of Thun. Although the local church records of Thurnen for the early 1700s no longer exist, civic records in Kerzers show that Johannes Etter sent word home to his *Heimatgemeinde* (the community to which the family legally belonged) to register the baptisms there of his two eldest children, Daniel, born in 1713, and Peter, born in 1715. After a few years in Riggisberg in the farming country of the lower foothills of the Alps, the family moved to the village of Munchenbuchsee near the capital city of Switzerland, Bern. There, Johannes Etter became an innkeeper. In Munchenbuchsee two children were born, Johannes Junior, in 1723, and Samuel, in 1724.

Growing up in an inn near Bern seems to have brought certain advantages to Peter Etter. With urban life came the possibility of an education, for documents show that in his later life he was able to thrive in the business life of Philadelphia and Boston. As Munchenbuchsee was situated near the "language border" and some of the guests at the family inn were French-speaking, he became bilingual. This aided him in later years in Boston, where he was made an official interpreter of French and German to the British authorities. Living in an inn, the Etter family had many opportunities to learn the news of the countryside, and during the 1720s and, in particular, the 1730s, much of the news concerned the large number of Swiss who were emigrating to America. As a man who was already uprooted from the farm where his family had lived for generations, Johannes was willing to consider moving once again, this time to America.

There was a considerable amount of unrest in Bern at the time. The government of the period was despotic. In fact, the period 1648–1798 has become known as the Age

A view of the interior of the parish church of Thurnen, showing
characteristic church furnishings of the eighteenth century.

of the Aristocracy. Difficulties were put into the way of those who wanted to become burghers, or members of the middle class, and they were excluded from the government. A few hundred families in the capital town of Bern held great power and attempted to keep from sharing this with newcomers, closing any chance of political office to the mass of the people of the canton. In addition, a barrier was erected between the people of the town of Bern and the country folk. Anyone who was fortunate enough to have been born in one of the burgher families of Bern was a hereditary lord and burgher while one born in the rural districts was a hereditary subject and must submit to the laws made by the burghers. In addition, they as subjects had to pay taxes to their hereditary lords in Bern. Many of the people of the canton objected to the control and taxes placed on them, and wished to emigrate to America.

Among those who particularly wished to emigrate were Mennonites who were not considered acceptable because of their religious beliefs and were, to some degree, even persecuted. They were encouraged by the authorities to join their fellow brethren from the Palatinate down the Rhine, and to emigrate to America. However, other Swiss were discouraged from emigration. In fact, it was considered a crime to incite others to leave for America. Those permitted to emigrate were taxed. Nevertheless, encouraging letters coming from both South Carolina, where a Swiss colony had been established early in the eighteenth century, and in particular from Pennsylvania, sent a steady stream of Swiss immigrants to America. They were attracted by the promises of William Penn (1644–1718) whose prospectus *Some Accounts of the Province of Pennsylvania* ... presented glowing accounts of the healthful climate, political and religious freedom, peace, and economic opportunity of life in Penn's colony in America.

The people of the Palatinate left chiefly as refugees whose lands had been ravaged in the dynastic wars fought in their territory in the name of religion. The reasons why Swiss of the Reformed religion would wish to leave their country were somewhat less obvious. Economics played a role; apart from farming or taking up one of the

*The baptismal font of the parish church in Thurnen in which Peter Etter was baptised in 1715.*

usual trades, membership in which was strictly in the hands of powerful guilds, the only occupation open to the ordinary citizen was as a mercenary in a foreign army. Peter Etter trained as a stocking weaver, Daniel and Johannes as tailors. As tradesmen, they were better off than most. But they were seemingly not averse to leaving Bern for Pennsylvania, since the prospects there seemed so much brighter than they were in Canton Bern.

The high point in this emigration from Bern was reached in the 1730s and 1740s, and it was then that the Etter family, too, went to America. Only the family in Munchenbuchsee of all the large Murten-Kerzers-Ferenbalm Etter connection emigrated at this period. And only Johannes Etter, the father of the family, emigrated in the beginning. He left in 1735, at the age of 55, travelling with a group of people from Munchenbuchsee. His first wife appears to have died, for she is not listed as going with him. In fact, her name last appears in the village records in 1724 at the time of the birth of her son, Samuel Etter. Instead of Anna Sigrist, Johannes Etter was accompanied by a "Margaret", presumably his second wife.

They travelled by the same route followed by other Swiss emigrants bound for America. First they went to the city of Basel, in the north of Switzerland. There, they arranged passage on a boat for the journey down the Rhine River to the sea, a beautiful but difficult and demanding trip which lasted two full weeks on the average, and meant frequent stops at small principalities where they were required to pay tolls before being allowed to proceed on their way. Shortly after leaving Basel, they passed through the region known as the Palatinate. There, the formerly rich and fertile farmlands had been devastated a generation earlier and many Palatinate Germans had left for new homes in Pennsylvania and New York State. Eventually, the party reached Rotterdam where they hired passage on the brig *Billander Olliver* bound for South Carolina and Philadelphia. They arrived at Philadelphia on 26 August 1735. Two years later, Peter Etter set out to join his father. Finally, in 1742, upon the arrival in Philadelphia of Daniel and Johannes Junior, the Etter family was reunited. Only one son, Samuel, was

*Swiss emigrants such as the Etters made their way to Basel, on the Rhine. There they found accommodation on a river boat to take them down the Rhine.*

*After some weeks of travel they reached Rotterdam, a crowded seaport in the Netherlands where they could negotiate for passage to America.*

seemingly left behind in Switzerland, but it is more likely that he had died in childhood, since his name does not appear in the records of Munchenbuchsee after his birth was recorded in 1624.

In Pennsylvania the Etters soon received land from William Penn, Johannes obtaining four land grants between 1737 and 1743. These were located in Donegal Township in Lancaster County where Johannes and his younger son, Johannes Junior, farmed. Daniel and Peter, the older sons, did not take up farming but stayed in Philadelphia. There, Daniel became an innkeeper, owning an inn located near Second and Race Streets for many years. Peter lived nearby in a house where he set up his stocking looms. Both brothers had taken their oath of allegiance to the King of England immediately upon arrival in Philadelphia, and they were both naturalized as British citizens together in that same city on 1 June 1749. It appears that during this period they changed their religion. Between the time of their arrival in 1737 and in 1742, when neither of them had hesitated to swear an oath of allegiance, and 1749, when they claimed religious scruples about swearing any oath, they had become Moravians. Consequently, they were allowed to subscribe to, rather than swear to, the terms of naturalization, as did Quakers and others who followed literally the Biblical teaching to "swear not at all."

The Etters had been members of the Reformed Church in Switzerland, but in Pennsylvania all members of the family were converted by ministers of the Unitas Fratrum of Moravian Brethren, the oldest Protestant Episcopal church, founded in 1457 by followers of John Hus in Bohemia. A few missionaries of the Brethren came to Pennsylvania about the same time as the Etters, and set about establishing a retreat for persecuted members of their faith. They also began to serve as missionaries to the Indians, in particular, the Delawares and to convert many German-speaking immigrants who were drawn by their gentleness and piety. The Moravian church was given full acceptance by the Anglican Church in America, and Moravians often became Anglicans in the absence of a church of their own denomination.

110

*The stocking frame, a machine on which long cotton, wool, or silk stockings could be knit, was invented in England by an unknown inventor, and became one of the proto-industrial machines of the textile trades. The knitter's assistant is seen winding hanks of silk thread onto the special bobbins used in this frame. The model shown is one widely used in the eighteenth century, similar to those used by Peter Etter in Braintree.*

Peter Etter soon owned a small factory of several looms and within ten years of his arrival in Philadelphia had become a well-known business man, married, with a young family. The War of the Austrian Succession (1740–1748) was in progress at the time and had spread to the British colonies in America where it was called King George's War (1744–1748). French and Spanish privateers raided up the Delaware, although not as far up as Philadelphia. However, in 1747 such a raid was considered a distinct threat and Philadelphia was completely undefended and vulnerable. Benjamin Franklin led a movement to raise troops for defence, but this was strongly opposed by the Quakers who controlled a majority in the Pennsylvania Assembly and who were strictly pacifist. The government would not agree to supply funds for the military, but in December 1747 Franklin succeeded in raising an association of volunteers who outfitted themselves with personal funds, by subscription dances, and by public lotteries. Peter Etter was one of the officers, elected an ensign or second lieutenant, and his commission was later confirmed by the Provincial Council on 1 January 1748. This military unit, known as the Philadelphia Associators, established two forts with heavy guns on the Delaware, and took turns manning these forts. They were never involved in actual battle during King George's War, although their defence of Philadelphia may have prevented an attack. When hostilities ended in August 1748, the Associators disbanded. Peter Etter remained a friend of the Franklin family, and a business associate of Benjamin Franklin's brother, John.

About 1750, Peter Etter moved to Braintree, Massachusetts, near Boston, where he again set up in business. He became the official British translator for the French and German speaking refugees who continued to arrive in the British colonies in great numbers. Soon he became associated with John Franklin, Joseph Crellius, Isaac Winslow, and Norton Quincy in a plan to establish an industrial settlement in Braintree, a community of German-speaking artisans whose first project would be to establish a glass factory.[1] The five Boston businessmen drew plans for a community to be called Germantown, surveyed into lots, streets, and squares named after familiar towns and cities of Europe, such as Bern Square. It was probably this plan for an industrial complex which Benjamin Franklin had in mind when he wrote to his brother John Franklin on 27 September 1750:

> We shall look over the Town Plan tomorrow (Mr. Etter and I) and if I can think of any Thing that may be advantageous, shall advise.[2]

Building operations soon began in Braintree where the group of businessmen established chocolate mills, spermaceti and glass works, salt manufacturing, and Peter Etter's stocking factory. The stocking factory prospered, but the glass works was a failure, although at first there was great hope that it would be successful. On 26 November 1753 John Franklin wrote to his brother Benjamin:

> Our furnice stands well at present and the Glassmen are fulley Employd in makeing Window Glass and Bottles. The former made of our own Materials is Light and Cleere beyond our Expectation so that we Expect it will be thought Good Enough to Glaize the New Church.[3]

Eventually, the associates sold the glass works to other owners and Peter Etter was no longer involved in the venture. He continued to manage his own stocking factory in Braintree, however, and this proved to be profitable. He became supplier to the British army, weaving stockings for the soldiers. He was well thought of in Braintree and on 2 March 1772 was one of the six people elected to be a warden of the town.

Etter became a good friend of John Adams who was later to become the second president of the United States and was mentioned several times in Adams' diary between 1760 and 1772.[4] However, Peter Etter was openly pro-royalist, while John Adams was anti-royalist and they had many arguments about such issues as the Stamp Act. On 29 May 1760 Adams wrote in his diary that Peter Etter had explained to him how his looms functioned, but that it was too complicated for him to understand. Six years later the two men, in spite of growing political differences,

113

*This cartoon published in 1774 illustrates the political upheaval in Boston in that year when the growing anger of the rebels led to persecution of those loyal to the Crown, culminating in the events of 1775-1776.*

were still good friends. On 12 January 1766, John Adams wrote in his diary "at Evening Mr. Etter, here." Two months later he wrote that Peter Etter and his own brother, Peter, had gone about Braintree gathering enough votes to succeed in getting him (John Adams) elected to be a select man of the town. A week later, he wrote that he had taken tea with Peter Etter. As the political tension grew, this friendship grew more difficult to maintain. Only two months after he wrote of his friendly encounters with Peter Etter, John Adams noted in his diary on 4 May 1766 that for the first time a "liberty tree", a place where rebels would assemble and advocate active rebellion, had been raised in Braintree, "by the house of James Brackett. The tree is well set, well guarded, and has on it an inscription, 'The tree of Liberty, and cursed is he who cuts this tree!' . . . I hear that some persons grumble, and threaten to girdle it." James Brackett was Peter Etter's frequent opponent in civic matters, and a leading rebel.

In Braintree there was a strong Tory element, and when the Stamp Act was repealed in 1766 there was no public demonstration of joy as there was in many of the towns of Massachusetts where rebels celebrated with great fervour. In the next few years, however, Braintree citizens' support for the rebels grew. Peter's second wife, Elizabeth Veazie (1733–1768), whom he married in 1755, a year after the death of his first wife, Margaret, belonged to a Tory family. The Veazies and many other fellow Episcopalians remained loyal to the King. Peter Etter was by now attracting attention as a leading Loyalist. Adams wrote in his diary: "Drank tea at Mr. Etter's. He said all the blame is laid to him, and that a certain man takes it very ill of him." In 1774 the growing political turmoil brought the Etters into real danger. John Adams's wife has recorded the following episode in 1774:

> About eight o'clock, Sunday evening, there passed by here about two hundred men, preceded by a horse cart, and marched down to the powder-house, from whence they took the powder, and carried it into the other parish, and there secreted it. I opened the window upon their return. They passed without any noise; not a word among them till they come

against this house, when some of them, perceiving me, asked me if I wanted any powder. I replied, No, since it was in so good hands. The reason they gave for taking it was, that we had so many Tories here they dared not trust us with it; they had taken Vinton in their train (Vinton was Sherreff under the Provincial Government), and upon their return they stopped between Cleverly's and Etter's and called upon him to deliver two warrants, (which were probably for them, as they were susposed to have been royalists). Upon his producing them, they put it to vote whether they should burn them, and it passed to the affirmative. They then made a circle and burnt them.[5]

Peter Etter was called before the Committee of Observation, of which James Brackett was a member and "asked to explain his conduct." On this occasion, "the relation Mr. Peter Etter made respecting his conduct is satisfactory to the town," was the final verdict. However, by January 1775 the Etter family was forced to flee to Boston as refugees.

Boston was still under the protection of British forces, and the Etters were temporarily safe after their arrival there. Tory refugees continued to crowd into the town which could barely house all the destitute newcomers. Peter Etter, his sons Peter and Franklin, and his brother Daniel, all joined the defence forces of beleaguered Boston. On 3 May 1775 they met with a large group of Tory citizens to make the following statement:

A number of the Loyal Subjects of the Province of Massachusetts Bay now residing in Boston, having met to deliberate and concert measures upon the alarming state of the Town proceeded to act thereon . . . (and) selected a committee to draft the form of a Association to be entered into and subscribed by such people as are now resident in the Town for maintaining peace and the support of the Government. We the subscribers considering the present Alarming situation of the Town being now invested by a large body of the people of the Country, and at all times ready to do all in our power for the support of the Government and good order and to

116

*Built in 1750, St. Paul's Church is the oldest existing building in Halifax, where it was built at the south end of the Grand Parade. This engraving of Halifax in 1759 by Richard Short shows the church as it appeared to Peter Etter and his family when they became active members upon their arrival in Halifax in 1776.*

resist all Lawless Violence, Have voluntarily assembled together and do mutually engage each with the other by this Subscription, That in the Case the Town should be attacked or assaulted or things brought to such emergencies as that our Aid may be thought necessary by the General that we will upon proper notice Assemble together and being supplied with proper Arms and Ammunition will contribute all in our power for the Common safety in Defense of the Town

(signed, together with other names)

Daniel Etter
Francklin Etter
Peter Etter
Peter Etter Junr.[6]

In March 1776 the British evacuated Boston, and Peter Etter and his family, in total a party numbering seven, were taken with some 1,100 other refugees to Halifax. Together with the British troops, they were brought in a number of brigs to an unprepared small port with little shelter, to a community described by one writer as follows:

Halifax, in 1776, was little more than a hamlet; at best, it was a miserable village, inhabited chiefly by fishermen. It was with difficulty such an accession to the stated population could be temporarily accommodated with shelter, fuel, and food; most of the houses were in a dilapidated state letting in the bleak winds of the season through manifold chinks, hardly a room having ever known the luxury of being plastered. Whole families were more uncomfortably crowded together than they had been in the few store-ships which had transported them from Boston.[7]

The refugees from Boston arrived in Halifax on 17 March 1776. Peter Etter decided to stay there and spent the last 18 years of his life as a citizen of the growing town. For several years, while he was in his 60s, he was employed as a messenger of the Nova Scotia House of Assembly. Meanwhile, his son Peter became a member

118

of the Royal Fencible American Regiment which served in Nova Scotia throughout the American Revolution. Afterwards, he became a jeweller and settled first in Halifax and later in Westmorland, where he founded a branch of the Etter family. A second branch was founded in Chester by Franklin Germanus Etter, named after Peter's friends, the Franklin family. He settled there after the close of the Revolution when he was released from service in the army. The third branch remained in Halifax where Benjamin Etter, Peter's youngest son also became a jeweller and silversmith.

On 14 July 1786 Peter Etter, with his son Peter Junior as a witness, appeared before Commissioner Pemberton at Halifax to make his claim for compensation. The official record of the evidence they presented states:

A New Claim

573. Case of Peter Etter, Sen., late of Massts.

Claimant Sworn Saith.

He sent his claim home to Rashleigh & Co. in Octr., 1783. It appears by a Letter from Rashleigh & Co., dated in Feby., 1784 in which they acknowledge they had recd. it.

Says he is a Swiss by birth, settled in America in the yr. 1737 first at Philadelphia, then went & settled at Braintree, Massts., 10 miles from Boston, in Business when Troubles broke out. He took ye King's Part & tried to advise his neighbours to do the same, for four months was obliged to quit his home.

In January, 1775 all his family removed to Boston & he continued to live there, came away with the Troops on Evacuation. Had 3 Sons in the Army, left his Stocking Frames with Tools, &c. at his House in Braintree, could not take them away, left his stock.

Was in Possession of 7 acres & 1–4, with house & builds. at Braintree, bought of Danl. Marsh for £100, some years before ye War. Built a house & bar[n], cost him £160 Ster. Vals. it at £250 Ster.

Claimt. says he owed £106.8 Str., & gave the Title Deed of this Estate to one Braket to secure him this money. He is now in Possession.

3 acres & 1/2 belonging to his wife. This has not been seized because it belongs to his children.

Frames & Tools in his house at Braintree now in Possession of Braket, cannot tell what right he has. He was one of the Committee of Safety, cost him 1,000 dollars. Vals. at £228 Ster.

Braket has let the Frames & part of the house. A Chaise left with his Brother in Law at Braintree.

Lost several articles on coming away from Boston, furniture, Cloaths of himself & children, the Packages were on the Wharf & could not be put on Board. Thinks they were all stole in the night, before the Ships fell down. Worth £93.

Lost 933 Pd. Indigo. It was bought by his Son who had the Charge of it. His son was prest into the American Service & obliged to leave the case of Indigo, &c., but it was taken Charge of by Ephraim Spooner. Says Spooner was a Rebel. Indigo worth 6sh. 6d. per pd. 72 Deer Skins worth 6sh. 30 otter skins worth 14sh. a small box of raw silk, all these articles were put in Mr. Spooner's Store.

Peter Etter, Jr., Wits.

Says he lived with his Father at Braintree, his Father from the first took part with the Brit. Was employed in making stockings for the Brit. Troops. He was mobbed & thinks he was obliged to go to Boston, on acct. of his Loyalty. He was obliged to make his escape from his house at Braintree, left one son in Possession, but the whole family were afterwards driven into Boston. His father continued in Boston till Evacuation.

The Estate at Braintree was bought of one Marsh, consisted of 7 acres & Quarter. His father built an house, out houses. It was mortgaged to one Braket. Braket is now in Possession. Braket is in Possession of Frames & Tools. Claimt. left his son in Possession, but he was obliged to come away & did not dare to return. So that the Stock as well as frames & Tools were all taken Possession by Braket. Imagines he took them under pretence of the Debt from his Father. Braket now lets part of the House, the Tools & frames to one Hardwick, who was Journeyman to Claimt. & now carries on the Trade.

*Peter Etter's granddaughter, Anna Sophia Verge (or Virgie) about 1870. She was the daughter of Sarah Verge, who was ten years old when the Etter family was evacuated with the British Army as Loyalist refugees in March 1776, and brought to Halifax. Anna Verge married a Scottish immigrant farmer, George Moffat, and settled in River Hebert, Nova Scotia.*

Remembers the loss of the things, lost from the wharf at time of Evacuation, when Things were in such disorder, Cloathing, Linen, & vars. articles, 3 or 4 Trunks, thinks must be worth £100. The Indigo &c. were in Witness Charge, he brought them from S. Carolina to Plimouth, in a schooner belonging to one Harlow, 2 Days before the Battle of Lexington. Witness went to see after his Father, being obliged to go with American Militia. Could not return to take care of Indigo. The owners of the Ship carried the things to Spooner's Store. He wrote to Witness's Sister to come & take Possession. Witness neglected going out for it, says he might have saved them, if he had gone out. He was advised not to go, does not know what is become of it.

John Miller, Wits

Knew Claimt. at Braintree. He always took part with the King & was obliged to leave his Estate on that Acct. & took Refuge at Boston, came from Boston at Evacuation.[8]

Peter Etter was allowed the sum of 70 pounds sterling of his total claim of 1,015 pounds sterling six shillings. Land grants were later made to the Etter family in Chester and in Cumberland County.

The records of St. Paul's Church, the Anglican church which the Etter family attended in Halifax, show that Peter Etter was buried in St. Paul's Burying Ground on 28 June 1794 at the age of 79. Little has been recorded of the last few years of his life. Much more is known of the life of his youngest son, Benjamin, who married three times and was the father of 19 children. He was one of the first watchmakers and jewellers in Halifax. According to tradition, he received his training as a silversmith, jeweller and watchmaker in Bern, Switzerland, returning from there in 1783. Certainly the examples of his work which may be seen in the Provincial Museum of Nova Scotia indicate that he was a skilled craftsman, one who carried on the Swiss tradition of excellence which he inherited from his father. Peter Etter may well have sent his youngest son back to the old country for the training which a young pioneering land could not yet provide.[9]

# Chapter Seven

# Abraham A. Rapelje
# (1772–1859)
# A Loyalist of
# French Huguenot Origin

*From the time when New Netherland became an English colony in 1664, the Rapelje family of Long Island was completely loyal to the Crown. An ancestor of the Rapeljes had fled France as a Huguenot in the sixteenth century, and had found refuge in the Northern Netherlands. From there, his descendants had emigrated to America with others who were persuaded to settle in New Netherland by the Dutch West Indian Company. Many of their fellow settlers were also religious refugees from various parts of war-torn Europe. After intermarriage with Dutch colonists, eventually the Rapelje family became Dutch in language and custom. As Loyalists in Canada they were closely associated with others of Dutch origin, among them the Van Allen and Wyckoff families who also settled in Norfolk County.*

By the middle of the sixteenth century, the Reformation had taken a strong foothold in France and the Huguenots, as the Protestants were called, were a powerful party with 2,140 churches in the country. There were many outbreaks of violence as Catholics and Huguenots clashed, and eventually these turned into outright armed combat. Many Huguenots left the country to find refuge in the Northern Netherlands, a haven for Protestants of that period.

Among the refugees who fled to the Netherlands was Gaspard Coley de Rapalje who was born in France at Chatillon-sur-Loire in 1505.[1] He was made a colonel of infantry in 1545 and served in the French forces for many years. He became a Protestant and because of this, three years later in 1548, his commission was taken away from him. He fled to safety in Holland. There he married the

123

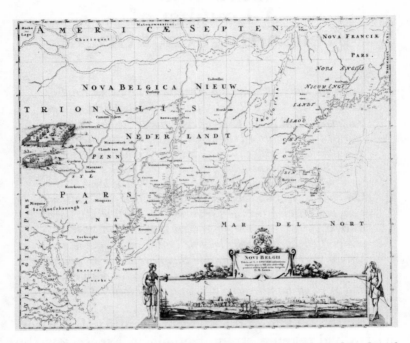

*New Amsterdam about the year 1750 is pictured in this detail
from a map of New Netherland by N. J. Visscher. The Rapelje
family traces its origins in America to this Dutch colonial capital
of the seventeenth century.*

daughter of another refugee, Victor Antonie Janssen, a house painter from Antwerp. They had three children, the second of whom, Abram, married a daughter of Hans Lodewyck in 1594, and had three sons, all of whom eventually emigrated to America. The eldest brother, Willem Janssen de Rapalje, left first in 1623. He travelled with the commercial agent and Governor of New Netherland, Peter Minuit. Before he left, he tried to persuade his brothers Joris and Antonie to follow him; before long they decided to do so.

Just four days before setting sail on the ship *Eendracht* on 25 January 1624, Joris was married to a refugee from Valenciennes, 18 year old Catalina Jeronimus Trico. There were a number of other Walloon and Huguenot families on the same ship so that they were able to continue to speak both French and Dutch, on board and after they arrived in America. They settled near their friends and fellow refugees at Beverwyck, a village developing at the fur post of Fort Orange (later Albany).

Joris had been a textile worker in Holland, but in New Netherland he worked at various occupations. At first, the work of the colonists was chiefly to bring the soil under cultivation and establish a permanent settlement. However, after the third harvest had been gathered at Beverwyck the Rapaljes, along with eight other families, were resettled in Manhattan by the West Indian Company. There, farms, a road system, building lots, and a fort were laid out and named New Amsterdam. The Rapaljes became one of the first families to settle there and, in fact, were said to be the parents of the first white child to be born in New Netherland, Sarah de Rapalje.

The youngest of the three brothers, Antonie Van Salers (so called because of a change of name as a result of inheriting property in France, in Salers in the Upper Auvergne), arrived in New Netherland in 1631 and settled at Gravesend on Long Island where he bought a 200 acre (80 hectares) property which was known as "Anthony Rapalje's Bowery" for many years, even after the British conquest of New Netherland. It was there that the eldest brother, Willem de Rapalje, died unmarried after serving for several years as a merchant of the West Indian Company.

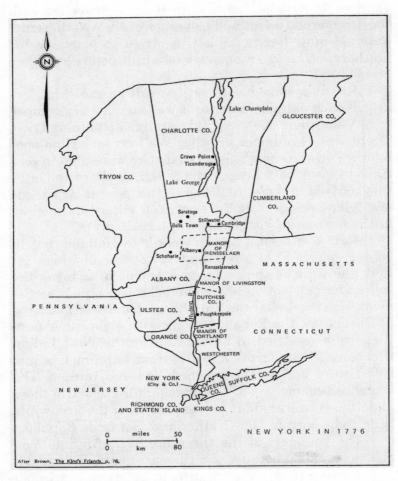

*New York as it appeared in 1776.*

Both Joris and Antonie had large families which continued to live on Long Island at Wallabout (originally Walenbocht, from the Dutch, meaning "the bay of the Walloons") nearly opposite New Amsterdam. Eventually, when each family had to select a permanent surname for legal purposes, the descendants of these families chose different names. The descendants of Joris chose "Jansen" as theirs, while those of Antonie dropped the "Jansen" of their original name and retained the Rapalje. The "Rapeljes" who came to Canada as Loyalists were thus descendants of Antonie rather than Joris, although the two families – the Jansens and the Rapeljes – continued to be closely knit by marriage and friendship in their community on Long Island and later as Loyalist refugees.

As the outbreak of the American Revolution became imminent, the Rapeljes' long-standing loyalty to the Crown was put to the test. In August, 1776, when the British fleet stood off New York and the army of George Washington was gathering there for its defence, angry rebels turned on the Loyalists who still remained there. Among these Tories was Jeromus Rapelje of Newton, Long Island, a militia captain and the grandfather of Abraham A. Rapelje. Contemporary accounts mention the ordeals Jeromus faced that year, which led to his death some months later.

As a nineteenth-century historian has commented:

> 'We had some grand Tory rides in the city this week,' Peter Elting wrote approvingly on the 13th to Richard Varick, 'and in particular yesterday. Several of them were handled very roughly, being carried through the streets on rails, their clothes torn from their backs, and their bodies pretty well mingled with the dust. Amongst them were C———'
> Captain Hardenbrook, Mr. Rapelje, . . . McQueen, the apothecary; and Lessly, the barber. There is hardly a Tory face to be seen this morning.'
> The Moravian pastor, Shewkirk, notes in his journal the same day: 'Here in town very unhappy and shocking scenes were exhibited. On Monday night some men called Tories were carried and hauled about through the streets with candles forced to be held in their faces and their heads burned; but on Wednes-

day, in the open day, the scene was far worse, several,
and among them gentlemen, were carried on rails,
some stripped naked and dreadfully abused. Some
of the generals, and especially Putnam, and their
forces, had enough to do to quell the riot, and make
the mob disperse.'

Another Loyalist, writing from Staten Island,
states that 'the persecution of Loyalists continues
unremitted. Donald McLean, Theophilus Harden-
brook, young Fueter, the silversmith, and Rem Rapelje, of Brooklyn, have been cruelly rode on rails,
a practice most painful, dangerous, and, till now,
peculiar to the humane Republicans of New England.[2]

Soon after this, the British forces landed and fought
on Long Island, afterwards taking possession of the city
of New York, which they held for nearly seven years. The
majority of its citizens welcomed them. Long Island was
said to have the greatest portion of Loyalists of any part
of the province of New York. Once the British were in
control, the Rapelje family were in a somewhat safer position. However, one of its members, John Rapelje, left
the country during the war and was reported to have gone
to either New Brunswick or Nova Scotia. His estates were
seized and sold about 1785. The Roblee family of New
Brunswick believe that they are descended from John
Rapelje and that he emigrated to Bear River, Nova Scotia
to found the Roblee (Rublee) family.

One of the members of the Rapelje family, Jeromus
Rapelje's son Abraham, died in 1780 leaving a wife and
two children, Abraham A. Rapelje, and Winnifred Rapelje
who was several years older than her brother. She was
married at 16 to Henry Van Allen who had served in the
Commissariat Department during the American Revolution. As Loyalists, the Rapelje family and their relatives, including the Van Allens, Abraham A. Rapelje, and
their mother, who had remarried and was the wife of a
Loyalist officer, Captain Vanderburg, went to Nova Scotia to settle.

On 14 August 1784, Ensign Henry Van Allen was
granted Crown land, and it appeared they would remain
there in Nova Scotia. However, after about ten or eleven

years of hardship they all returned to Long Island. It is believed that they returned because they had discovered that since he was a minor, not all of Abraham A. Rapelje's property had been seized, and there was a possibility of regaining some of it. It is quite possible, too, that like many other Loyalists they felt drawn back to their former homes when the political situation was more settled, hoping that their friends and relatives would welcome them and they could remain there peaceably. In any case, the family spent a few years on Long Island where Abraham and his brother-in-law Henry Van Allen were business partners.

In 1796, while still in New York State, Abraham married Sarah, daughter of Peter Wyckoff. Then, as "late Loyalists," in 1800, Abraham travelled to the province of Upper Canada with his wife and eldest daughter, the Van Allens and their children, his stepfather Captain Vanderburg (who was by then a widower) and his family, and two cousins, Daniel and Jeromus Rapelje. This group of immigrants went to Norfolk County which was then being settled, and took up land at Dover Mills, now Port Dover. A careful record of the various moves made by this Loyalist family was prepared by one of the children of Abraham A. Rapelje, Mrs. Charles Strange Perley of Port Dover who was active as a member of the United Empire Loyalists' Association of Ontario at the end of the nineteenth century. At that time, the so-called "late Loyalists" were often pictured in a bad light.

Mrs. Perley was able to remember details told by her parents of their early deprivations as Loyalists in Nova Scotia, and could explain their late arrival. Another descendant, Agnes E. R. Taylor of Hamilton, has commented on this controversy:

> These particulars are made very clear, because the 'late Loyalists,' especially those who settled in the County of Norfolk, have been held up in a very uncomplimentary light in an article written by a member of the U. E. L. Association; their motive for seeking refuge in Canada having been ascribed to gain. This certainly cannot be said of Abraham A. Rapelje, for he had sufficient to make a start with in the new

129

*The Battle of Lundy's Lane, in which Abraham A. Rapelje took part, while serving as a captain in the Norfolk Militia. He was active in this capacity throughout the War of 1812.*

country, and did not receive an acre of ground from the Government when he settled here. His reason for coming was solely that he might live under British rule.[3]

The Rapeljes and the Van Allens were still living at Dover Mills in the summer of 1812 when war broke out. Abraham A. Rapelje became a captain in the Norfolk Militia, serving in this capacity from 1812–1814. The notebook which he carried all through the war was preserved by his family and later descendants and is now held in the manuscript collection of the Archives of Ontario. In it, one can read the names of the men under his command in two Muster Rolls, and also learn of the role he played in the War of 1812. According to his daughter, Mrs. Perley, he was prevented from taking part in the Battle of Queenston Heights on 13 October 1812 by severe illness, and lay at home in Dover Mills on sick leave, suffering from "fever and ague." After this battle, his company was sent first to Sugar Loaf, then to Fort Erie, where they fought on 28 November 1812. In his notebook, he recorded details of the engagement:

> Fort Erie, 28th November 1812. The Americans came over with a large number of boats. By examination of a witness we took says they [the Americans] could not collect more than 3000 men on the frontier, that 800 or 1000 attempted to land on 28th, inst., but could not effect their purpose, and they suffered severely by the brave few that opposed them, who were rightly but few in number in comparison to the Americans, who made the best of their way back with their shattered boats, after leaving a number dead, and some prisoners, perhaps 50.[4]

Later he wrote, "I returned from Long Point to Burlington, October 29th, 1813, and joined the Company at Stoney Creek that night." The Battle of Stoney Creek had already been fought at this time, however, and it is likely that he and his men were elsewhere on the Niagara frontier in June of 1813 when this battle took place. According to his daughter, Mrs. Perley, he fought at Lundy's Lane and later at Fort Erie. Meantime, his wife went to York (now Toronto) with other officers' wives, and nursed the wounded.

When the war was over, in accordance with the regulations of the time, he drew half-pay to the time of his death in 1859. Eventually, he settled with his family at Vittoria which was then, in 1814, the chief village in the County of Norfolk and growing rapidly. He brought carpenters from New York to build the large home, "Oak Lodge," which he constructed on a farm lot of 100 acres (40 hectares). In 1818 he was appointed Sheriff of the London District, and held this office for 31 years. He long remained active in the Norfolk Militia. Both he, as colonel, and his son, as captain, were on active service in the Rebellion of 1837.

Abraham A. Rapelje's wife kept in contact with her family, the Wyckoffs of Long Island. In fact, on at least two occasions she made the difficult journey from Vittoria to New York City to see them. Writing in 1899, a descendant has described these travels which were most unusual for the time:

> In these days of rapid transit, it may be of interest to look back a little less than a hundred years, and see how they travelled in Canada then. Mrs. Rapelje was filled with a great desire to see her mother, after she had lived here nearly twenty years; her husband could not go with her as his many duties kept him busy at that time, so she started out to drive to her home on Long Island in a light wagon, over which her husband built a canvas hood to protect them from the weather. She took with her her youngest daughter of less than a year old, and her son Abraham, a lad of sixteen years. It took them three weeks to make the trip from Vittoria; each night they spent at some house or stopping place on the way.
>
> In 1824 she again went to visit her old home, this time accompanied by her husband, and he brought back with him the first carriage to come into the County of Norfolk, with a pair of horses and silver-plated harness complete.
>
> Another way of travel was by water, going by bateaux from Port Ryerse to Buffalo, thence to Black

*Mrs. Perley, a daughter of Abraham A. Rapelje, was an active member of the United Empire Loyalists Association of Canada during its early years of existence. She is seen here in a photograph taken about 1900.*

Rock and from there by canal-boats to New York. These boats in those days were considered quite luxurious. It took them eleven days to make the trip from Black Rock to New York, as many stops were made, but they made the return in six.[5]

The old Wyckoff homestead on Long Island which the Rapeljes visited dated from 1635, and had been passed from generation to generation since that time. It had been in the Wyckoff family for nearly 200 years at the time of their visits early in the nineteenth century. The family property in Flatbush was said to have been bought from the Canarsie Indians by the original immigrant from Holland, Peter Wyckoff, one of the early farmers of New Netherland. This farm had prospered and was a fine, productive establishment in 1796 when Sarah Wyckoff left to marry Abraham A. Rapelje and to settle in the wilderness of Norfolk in 1800. It is not surprising that Sarah Rapelje wished to return to visit her former home where she had lived a life of comfort as a girl.

Upper Canada was developing at a rapid pace with new areas opening up as immigrants began to arrive in considerable numbers in the 1830s and 1840s. As new communities were established and the County of Norfolk developed, the children of the Rapelje, Wyckoff, and Van Allen families moved into pioneer districts and founded families of their own. Some of the children and grandchildren of the Van Allen family became early settlers in Chatham which began to grow rapidly in the 1830s. Soon they were active in business there and owned mills and shipbuilding works.

Over the years, descendants of the Rapeljes often changed the spelling of the family name eventually making use of such variants as Rapely and Rapelye, as well as the less recognizable forms of Roblee and Rublee, used by their relatives in Nova Scotia and New Brunswick. All of these names can be traced back to the original name of Rapalje, used in the seventeenth and eighteenth centuries by their ancestors in New Netherland. This Dutch name is a reminder of the years which the Rapelje family's forefathers spent first as refugees in the Northern

134

Netherlands, and later as settlers in New Netherland. When Abraham A. Rapelje entered Canada as a "late Loyalist" in 1800, he came as an immigrant of part Dutch, part French Huguenot descent.

*Detail from a portrait of Flora Macdonald by Allan Ramsay, from the collection of the Ashmolean Museum, Oxford.*

# Chapter Eight

## Flora Macdonald
## (1722–1790)
## A Loyalist from the Scottish Highlands

*Fionnghal nighean Raonuill 'ic Aonghais Oig, better known under her anglicized name of Flora Macdonald, is remembered as the young heroine who helped Prince Charles escape his enemies after the Jacobite defeat at Culloden. During the American Revolution, Flora and her husband lived in a settlement of Scottish Highlanders in North Carolina. Caught up in the Revolution, as Loyalist supporters of King George, the Macdonalds came to Nova Scotia. While her husband served as a British officer, Flora lived for some time at Windsor, Nova Scotia, before eventually returning to Scotland.*

Fionnghal means "the fair one" in Gaelic, and Flora was the English name chosen to express this meaning. It suited Flora Macdonald who was a modest, sincere woman of great charm and of fair complexion. She was known for her practical nature and sense of humour. Flora was the only daughter of Ranald Macdonald of Milton and Belvannich in the Outer Hebrides. They lived on the Roman Catholic island of South Uist, her father's island. On her father's side of the family she was a descendant of the Captains of Clanranald, while her mother was a Macdonald of North Uist, the daughter of an Episcopalian clergyman. Flora herself was also an Episcopalian.

Flora's father was a *tacksman* who managed a number of farms. In the Scottish Highlands at that time the clan chiefs, who were the lords and landowners, seldom actually engaged in farming themselves. Instead they usually lived in Edinburgh and leased the lands to others. These men, known as tacksmen, acted as middlemen and in turn leased farms to sub-tenants in long-term leases

137

or "tacks." Sometimes, as in the case of Flora Macdonald's father, the tacksman owned the farm himself and let out part of the farm to many *cottars*, poor farmers to each of whom was given a house, enough grass to keep a cow or two, and a small plot of land on which to grow oats. This was the cottars' payment for their labour on the farm.

When Flora was two years old her father died, and her widowed mother married Hugh Macdonald of the Isle of Skye. Flora and her brother Angus were taken to Skye to live with their step-father and mother. When Angus came of age and inherited the family property of Milton on South Uist, Flora went to live with him there, although she continued to return to Skye from time to time and eventually married Allan Macdonald of that island. Throughout her life, South Uist remained her favourite island and she lived there through choice. However, she travelled frequently and was familiar with other islands of the Hebrides, including Benbecula on which Clanranald maintained a large household at Nunton. She also visited Edinburgh where she lived with relatives for some months and perhaps received some of her education, which was an excellent one. She became fluent in English as well as her native Gaelic, and was able to read and write in both languages, as well as sing and play the harp.

In June 1746 Flora was staying at Nunton when news arrived that the defeated pretender to the throne, Prince Charles, had landed in Benbecula and was in hiding on the island, sought by his enemies, including large detachments of Hanoverian soldiers which swarmed over every island, determined to capture him. They were apparently supported by the Skye militia, but in fact few of these local soldiers actually wished to capture the Prince, whom they secretly supported. One of the captains of this force was Flora's step-father, Hugh Macdonald. He is believed to have been the originator of the idea by which the Prince's life was saved, by bringing him over to the mainland. In any case, Flora was chosen to execute this idea.

On 21 June Prince Charles set out to meet Flora Macdonald accompanied only by two loyal men. Flora had in the meantime gone up to the hills to stay in a *shieling* used only during the summer months, saying that she

*A print dating from the eighteenth century pictures life in a Scottish cottar's home in the Highlands.*

was helping her brother by looking for lost sheep in the hills. After walking cross-country for hours that night, the two supporters of the Prince reached the hut where Flora was waiting. They made final plans for Charles to make a desperate attempt to escape from the island, and so to save his life.

Captain Felix O'Neill, an Irish supporter of Prince Charles, has left his version of the meeting with Flora:

> At midnight we came to a hut, where by good fortune we met with Miss Flora MacDonald, whom I formerly knew. I quitted the Prince at some distance from the hut, and went with a design to inform myself if the Independent Companies were to pass that way next day. The young lady answered . . . that they would not pass till the day after. Then I told her I brought a friend to see her, and she, with some emotion, asked me if it was the Prince, I answered her it was, and instantly brought him in.
>
> We then consulted on the imminent danger the Prince was in, and could think of a no more proper and safe expedient than to propose to Miss Flora to convey him to the Isle of Skye, where her mother lived. This seemed the more feasible, as the young lady's father, being Captain of an Independent Company, would accord her a pass for herself and a servant to go visit her mother. The Prince assented, and immediately proposed it to the young lady, . . . she at length acquiesced, after the Prince had told her the sense he would always retain of so conspicuous a service.[1]

In the morning Flora set out for the Clanranald's house but was stopped by soldiers because she did not have a pass. Then she discovered that the commanding officer of this particular group was her own step-father, who was away but would soon return. From him she obtained a pass for herself, another woman, and a man-servant. The woman's name was given as Betty Burke, for it was decided that Charles would make his escape to the Isle of Skye using this name and disguised as a servant.

*During the summer months in the Highlands the cattle were driven into the hills to the shielings, stone huts built by the shepherds where they lived during the months of good weather. It was in such a setting that Flora Macdonald met messengers from Prince Charles.*

Prince Charles, meanwhile, was helped by Lady Clanranald, who had servants spend two days creating a woman's costume for him.[2]

On 28 June the disguised Prince Charles, Flora, Neil Mackechan, and four boatsmen set off for Skye. Flora travelled frequently between the islands and so had every reason to be expected to be going to Skye. However, when they tried to land at Waternish they found it occupied by the Hanoverian forces, who fired on them. They escaped, and managed to land at Kilbride where they found a sympathetic Jacobite woman, the wife of Sir Alexander Macdonald of Monkstat, who gave them shelter. This was not a safe refuge, and Prince Charles was soon sent to Sir Alexander's factor's house at Kingsburgh. However, the factor's wife soon became suspicious of the strange behaviour of Betty Burke: "I never saw such an odd muckle trollup of a carlin making lang wide steps through the hall, that I could not like her appearance at all."[3] Thereupon she was told that she was entertaining Prince Charles. However, he kept his disguise until after leaving Kingsburgh on 30 June, at which time he changed back into Highland dress. Flora and the Prince then travelled by different routes. Flora went to her family home at Armadale. Charles was given a guide to help him reach Portree, then taken to the Isle of Skye and the mainland. By September he had reached France. The Prince " . . . bid farewell to Miss Macdonald . . . 'I believe, Madam, I owe you a crown of borrowed money.' She said that it was only a half-crown, and he paid her this, with thanks. Then he saluted her and exclaimed: 'For all that has happened I hope, Madam, we shall meet in St. James's yet.' "[4] As a token of remembrance he gave her a blue French velvet garter which he had worn when disguised as Betty Burke. Earlier, at the Clanranald home, she had received a lock of his hair as a keepsake.

Flora and Prince Charles never met again. Soon afterwards, Flora was captured and taken as a prisoner to Dunstaffnage Castle. From there she was taken first to Edinburgh, then imprisoned on a troopship at Leith for a full 12 months before being taken to London. However, she was well treated and allowed to entertain her friends to dinner in the ship's cabin. The Scottish Jacobites, and

142

*Prince Charles was attended by two gentlemen who were his companions and aides during his flight, and helped him to escape his enemies with the cooperation of Flora Macdonald.*

even the English, considered her a heroine for the brave role she had played in the Prince's escape, so she was given great honour while she was in prison in Edinburgh, and eventually was released in London. Sympathetic friends there welcomed her to their home, and she visited London for some time before returning home to Skye. There, in 1750, she married Allan, the son of Sir Alexander Macdonald of Kingsburgh. He was not a Jacobite and had served in the Hanoverian army that defeated Prince Charles at Culloden.

For some time they lived at Flodigarry, and later at Kingsburgh. All told, seven children were born to Flora and Allan – Charles, named for the Prince (1751), Anne (1754), Alexander (1755), Ranald (1756), James (1757), John (1759), and Francis, known as Fanny (1766). In 1772 Sir Alexander died and Flora's husband inherited the Macdonald estate at Kingsburgh. However, economic conditions on the estate were poor and the family encountered financial difficulties. Flora and her husband, like many other Highlanders of the time, decided to emigrate to America.[5]

Not long before the Macdonalds left, in September 1773, they were visited by the famous English writer Dr. Samuel Johnson, who was accompanied by his biographer James Boswell. These travellers were struck by what Boswell called the Highland "rage of emigration." More than 2,000 people had recently left the Isle of Skye, and 200 were planning to follow, including Flora and her husband. Emigration was so popular an idea that a dance called "America," a fashionable reel, was featured at parties on Skye. The Macdonalds and their visitors attended parties where the dancers would move in circles which grew wider and wider until the dancing "emigrants" left the floor in couples and small groups. Boswell said, "It shows how emigration catches until all are set afloat."

There was a general discontent in the Highlands which rose to a high level in the years 1768 to 1773. After the defeat at Culloden, the government attempted to break down the clan system. In 1768 a large group of Highlanders was led by the tacksmen of Macdonald of Sleat to the Carolinas where they bought 100,000 acres (40,000 hectares) of land. Each year, many ships left for America,

*Prince Charles dressed as "Betty Burke", in which disguise he posed as Flora Macdonald's serving woman.*

carrying large groups of clansmen. Johnson wrote, "Many of considerable wealth have taken with them their train of labourers and dependants, and if they continue the feudal scheme of polity, they may establish new clans in the other hemisphere." Many were former Jacobites. All of them felt that the new world would offer better opportunities. Year after year, life was difficult in the Highlands, and in 1771 and 1772 the weather conditions brought disaster. That winter, violent storms drove more than 1,000 Highlanders to emigrate to North Carolina. The year 1773 marked the largest emigration to America up to that time, recorded as 3,169 although likely amounting to a much larger number, for accurate records were not kept at the time. In the 12 years ending in 1776, more than 23,000 Highlanders left for America.

Many of the emigrants to America had been Jacobites and were looking for both political and religious freedom:

> ... the unfortunate Prince Charlie landed at Moidart. The Catholics rose with him as one man. They fought heroically in his cause ... But, alas, England was too wealthy; the English soldiers were too numerous for them. And on Culloden moor, cold, famished, weary, and leaderless, they fell in hundreds before the cannons of the Southerners ....
>
> And, if the Catholics were persecuted before then, thereafter they were scarcely allowed to live .... But rather than forsake their faith the heroic confessors left the land of their love; they parted with their worldly goods; and they took their wives and children with them across the ocean to make new homes for themselves in the melancholy forests of America.[6]

In Scotland, the Reformation had not affected the entire country, and many of the inhabitants, particularly in parts of the Highlands and on certain islands, continued to worship as Roman Catholics. Many left to find a refuge in America, in North Carolina, on the Johnson estate in the Mohawk Valley of New York, or in Nova Scotia.

*This illustration, entitled "Flora Macdonald Assisting the Escape of the Pretender" was included in a favourite children's book of 1879 by C.D. Yonge,* The Seven Heroines of Christendom.

While about one-half of the Jacobite forces were Catholics, many of the active supporters of Prince Charles did not support the "old religion." Among these was Flora who, as a devout Anglican, took only her Prayer Book with her as reading matter when she was arrested and put into confinement on the prison-ship at Leith, although her friends secured a Bible for her use there. So it was not for religious reasons that Allan and Flora Macdonald decided to emigrate to America. Rather, their reasons were chiefly a search for political freedom and an escape from their financial problems, for they had fallen into debt during the harsh years which had just passed. They were strongly affected by the memory of the winter of 1771–72, the worst anyone in Scotland could remember, which had begun already on 2 September with frost and sleet. The storms had lasted through until April and whole herds of cattle had died:

> . . . crowds were passing emaciated with hunger, to the eastern coast, on the report of a ship being there, laden with meal. Numbers of the miserables of the country were now migrating; they wandered in a state of desperation; too poor to pay, they madly sell themselves for their passage, preferring a temporary bondage in a strange land to starving for life on their native soil. . . . . The people are almost torpid with idleness, and most wretched, their hovels miserable, made of poles wattled and covered with sods. There is not corn raised sufficient to supply the wants of the inhabitants.[7]

In the spring, a great famine struck Scotland. It is not surprising that like other emigrants, the Macdonalds were looking forward to the warm, pleasant climate of North Carolina, of which they had heard so much.

Yet they must have been aware that opportunities for education were few in the colonies, for they decided to leave the two youngest children behind. John, then 15, was placed in Edinburgh to attend school, and eight-year-old Fanny went to friends, possibly on the Isle of Raasay. Those who would accompany Flora and Allan were their sons Alexander and James, daughter Anne and her husband, Alexander Macleod of Glendale, and their two small sons, as well as eight indentured servants. Charles, the eldest, was employed by the East India Company, while Ranald, the third son, was serving as a lieutenant in the marines.

In August 1774 the Macdonald party sailed from Campbelltown in the *Balliol*, bound for North Carolina. On the open seas, their ship was attacked by a French privateer, and in the ensuing battle and confusion Flora was injured, her arm damaged. Upon safe arrival, Allan Macdonald bought a piece of land in the Scottish settlement in North Carolina and named it Killegray. There they settled, with the full intention of making a permanent home.

However, 1775 was "the year of decision" and times were troubled. Once again, Allan Macdonald chose to join the Hanoverian forces in support of King George III, as he had served in George II's army on former occasions during his highly adventurous life. As a Loyalist supporter of the Crown, he was commissioned a captain in the 2nd Battalion, Royal Highland Emigrants (later the 84th Regiment), made up of American Highlanders. The headquarters of the 1st Battalion were in Quebec City; those of the 2nd Battalion in Halifax. Allan's first duty was to go as a recruiting officer throughout the Scottish settlements of North Carolina, raising a body of Loyalists.

He was successful in raising troops and prepared to march north. His second son, Alexander, was given a commission as a lieutenant in the battalion. Setting out for Boston, where the battalion was to muster, they were caught in an ambush at Moore's Creek Bridge. Many were drowned or shot and others were taken prisoner. Among those captured were Allan Macdonald and his son Alexander, who were imprisoned at Halifax, Virginia. Their names are on a "List of North Carolina Loyalist Prisoners Destined for Philadelphia, Pa., as enclosed with a letter to the Continental Congress 22 April 1776." In this document, they are listed as "Colonel Allen McDonald, from Kingsborough, first in commission in Army and second-in-command, and Alexander McDonaldson from Kingsborough." In 1777 Allan and his son were exchanged for rebel prisoners, and sent from Philadelphia to the British garrison at New York City. There, Allan was given a temporary appointment under General Sir William Howe.

The following year, Allan was sent to headquarters in Halifax, Nova Scotia, where he was on duty for three years. Towards the end of the conflict he was sent to Cape Breton. During the war, four of Flora and Allan's sons served in regular or Loyalist forces. Alexander, nicknamed Sandy, may have been with one of the companies of Royal Highland Emigrants that were sent to fight in the southern colonies. Charles left the East India Company's service and ultimately received a captaincy in the British Legion, one of the most active of the Provincial Corps, in which James, the fourth son, was commissioned a lieutenant. Ranald, the second son, remained with the marines. When the revolution came to an end, Allan decided to return to Scotland rather than re-establish a home in America, although as a captain in the Royal Highland Emigrants, he was entitled to 5,000 acres (2,000 hectares) of land in Nova Scotia.

Flora, her daughter and grandsons remained for some time in North Carolina before making their way north to New York City and on to Nova Scotia as Loyalists. In 1778 Flora joined her husband in Halifax, and soon made a temporary home in Windsor, a small community which was directly connected with Halifax, where Allan was stationed for a while. After about a year and a half, however, she decided to return to Scotland, at least partly for reasons of failing health, and her daughter and grandchildren went with her. No doubt the whole family had decided to return to Scotland, and Flora went ahead, planning to await her husband there.

During the greater part of the time Allan was stationed in Nova Scotia, Flora lived in a small cottage which her brother built for her at Kildonan, in South Uist. Two letters tell of her life at this time. The first, dated July 1780 reads:

> I have pleasure to inform you, upon my arrival here, that I had two letters from my husband; the latter dated tenth May. He was then in very good health, and informs me that my son Charles has got the command of a troop of horse in Lord Cathcart's

regiment. But Alas! I have heard nothing since I left about my son Sandy, which you may be sure gives me great uneasiness; but I still hope for the best.

A second letter written two years later in July 1782 reads:

> I received a letter from Captain Macdonald, my husband, dated from Halifax, the twelfth of November, '81; he was then recovering his health, but had been very tender for some time before. My son Charles is captain in the British Legion, and James a lieutenant in the same: they are both in New York. Ranald is Captain of Marines, and was with Rodney at the taking of St. Eustatia. As for my son Sandy, who was amissing, I had accounts of his being carried to Lisbon, but nothing certain .... I am now at my brother's house, on my way to Skye, to attend my daughter, who is to lie-in in August; they are all in health at present.[8]

After long years of anxiety, Allan Macdonald returned to Scotland in 1784 when the forces were disbanded at the end of the Revolution. He joined Flora in the small cottage in South Uist. Later, they returned together to the Macdonald family estate at Kingsburgh on the Isle of Skye. There they spent the next few years in an attempt to manage the land Allan had inherited from his father in 1772, not long before leaving for America.

Flora Macdonald died at the age of 68, on a visit to the local minister's wife early in March 1790 when she was suddenly taken ill. To the local people, former Jacobites, Flora Macdonald was a heroine and not forgotten, and a great crowd gathered at the funeral ceremony at Kilmuir in Skye. Later, a tomb was erected in her honour. On it, Dr. Samuel Johnson's tribute to Flora was inscribed, for passers-by to read:

### Flora Macdonald

A name that will be mentioned in history, and if courage and fidelity be virtues, mentioned with honour. She is a woman of middle stature, soft features, gentle manners, and elegant presence.

Unfortunately, generations of tourists chipped away the stone on which these words were engraved. In 1860, the marble marker was removed and a tall Iona cross raised in memory of Flora Macdonald, an unforgotten heroine of the last uprising on behalf of the Royal Stuarts. Less publicized was the fact that her husband and four of her sons were commissioned officers, two of whom lost their lives at sea, and that Flora Macdonald, as a former settler in the British colonies, played a role in the Loyalist cause.

*This sketch, entitled "The Proposed Site of Charlotteville" and dating from about 1793-1795, was drawn by Elizabeth Simcoe, the wife of John Graves Simcoe who was the first lieutenant-governor of Upper Canada. A number of Loyalists, among them the Rapelje family, settled in this area at Long Point.*

*A restored mill called "Volmolen" dating from 1750, located near the village of Epen in the province of Limburg, in the southern part of the Netherlands near the Belgian border. This mill, typical of eighteenth century mills of Europe and America such as that operated by Henry Magee, is once again in working order, using waterpower to grind grain for local inhabitants.*

# Chapter Nine

# Henry Magee
# (c. 1741–1806)
# An Irish Miller and Merchant

*In 1773 Henry Magee, his wife and one child, landed at Philadelphia with the intention of settling in Pennsylvania. Caught up in the political turmoil they moved further inland to Perth Valley where, by 1775, Henry Magee had set up a mill and was grinding flour for the local farmers. For supporting the Loyalist cause, he was charged with treason and took to the mountains. Foiled in an attempt to join Butler's Rangers, he made his way to Philadelphia to join the British forces. Eventually, he and his family were reunited in Nova Scotia where they settled in Horton Corner, now Kentville, in the Annapolis Valley.*

In the seventeenth century the thrifty, hardy Scots were strongly encouraged to settle in the north of Ireland where the Plantation of Ulster was founded. During the rule of James I, King of Scotland, England, and Ireland, 23 new towns were laid out on a grid pattern and connected with roads, for Ulster then had virtually only the one town, Newry. A Protestant cathedral was built in 1628 in one of the new towns, Derry, which was settled by London merchant companies and renamed Londonderry.

By 1640 there were about 40,000 Scottish settlers in Ulster, most of them Presbyterian. Among them were the ancestors of Henry Magee, whose family had been settled as "Planters" in Ireland for about a century at the time of his birth around the year 1741.

By the early eighteenth century the descendants of the Scottish immigrants, known in America as "Scotch-Irish," had increased in number and there was no longer enough land for their needs. Work became scarce, and unemployment a serious problem. In some cases, the

*Coupe sur la largeur*

*A cross section of an eighteenth century mill, showing the various operations of grinding grain for flour, an essential service in every pioneer community.*

landowners made life more difficult for their tenant farmers by making heavy financial demands on them. Many Scotch-Irish decided to emigrate to America where there would be an opportunity for advancement. In many cases, immigrants would follow friends and relatives, who encouraged them to come to America where closely-knit communities of people from the old country were being formed in the British colonies along the Atlantic seaboard. Many were interested in going to Pennsylvania where the Quaker William Penn's "Holy Experiment" had established a colony offering religious freedom and economic opportunity.

Like many others, Henry Magee of Armagh decided to sell his possessions in Ireland and sail for Pennsylvania. However, he went not as a Presbyterian or a member of the established Church of Ireland, but as a convert to a new religious movement, Methodism. He had become acquainted with the Reverend John Wesley who, with his brother Charles, was the founder of the Methodist movement, an effort to revitalize the established Anglican church. Wesley had called a prayer meeting in the community where Henry Magee lived and this was considered an affront by the local authorities. Magee was sent to break up the meeting. He listened to Wesley's preaching, but instead of dispersing the group he joined it. In fact, according to Henry Magee's great-grandchild, family tradition maintained that John Wesley became a friend and saw the Magee family off at the port of Londonderry when they sailed for America.[1]

In 1773 Henry Magee, his wife, and six-year-old son John, landed in Philadelphia. It appears that shortly after arrival Henry was struck with fever and before he had recuperated from his illness his wife gave birth to a second son who was named Henry. As soon as it became possible to do so the family left Philadelphia to move to Cumberland County where one Colonel Chambers was actively establishing a small community which was then called Chamberstown (later Chambersburg). Henry Magee stayed there only a short time before moving on to another community in the same county, the newly opened rural district of Perth Valley (now Path rather than Perth). There he settled with his family and established himself

157

as a miller. Soon he had leased a mill, had outfitted it at a cost of £150, and was grinding flour for the farmers of Perth Valley, a service which was essential in a small pioneering community.

For two years Magee worked as a miller in Perth Valley and "was often asked to join the Americans, but always refused. Never signed any Association." He was in an untenable position, a newcomer whose services as a miller were greatly needed but who steadily refused to join the rebels who formed the majority in the Valley. Consequently, he was "insulted, personally ill-treated & persecuted" during his two years of residence there. When war broke out his position worsened, and finally he was told to "grind flour for the poor at Boston." He refused, and was seized and accused of treason.

When as a Tory Henry Magee was brought before the rebel Council on a charge of treason, he had a surprising stroke of good luck. In the official documents of the case his name had been spelled incorrectly as "Maag" instead of Magee. Because of this error, the case was dismissed and the prisoner released. Magee fled to the mountains for safety. In doing so, he abandoned two properties, the mill and lands in Perth Valley and 300 acres (120 hectares) in Westmoreland County where he had bought land cheaply in 1774 soon after his arrival, promising to build a mill on it as part of the sale agreement. But he had not moved permanently to Westmoreland County since it was more profitable to continue to work in Perth Valley. Also, he had not built a mill "on account of the times."

While his wife and family stayed on in Chamberstown, Henry Magee joined about 30 friends in the mountains. By this time, in 1777, agents for Colonel John Butler were actively looking for recruits in the mountains of Pennsylvania. The small group of 30 men planned to join Butler's Rangers at Niagara and to urge others to come with them. Soon Magee and his friends had recruited 431 men and arranged for them to sign an agreement to join Butler's forces. However, one of their own men betrayed them and turned informer. The group was forced to disperse and a reward was offered for Henry Magee's life.

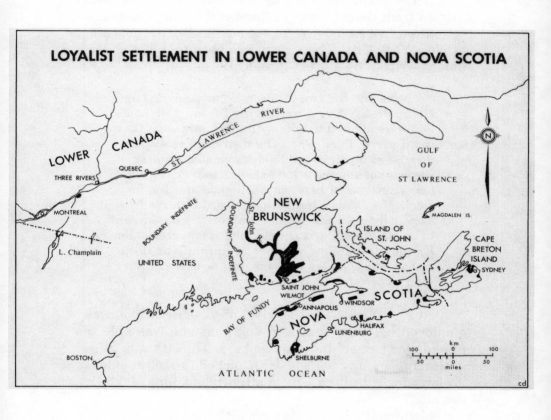

LOYALIST SETTLEMENT IN LOWER CANADA AND NOVA SCOTIA

Meanwhile, the British had occupied Philadelphia, and Magee managed to make his way there. He joined the British Army and remained in service for several years, attached to the Engineers' Department at a pay of five shillings per day. By 1778 he had come with part of the British Army to Nova Scotia.

In the meantime, his wife and two children had been evicted from their home in Chamberstown and forced to set out on foot as Tory refugees for the British garrison at New York City. Their story has been told in the document written by a great-grandchild:

> She and her two children, John aged nine and Henry Jr. aged two, were evicted from their home and were allowed to take with them only what they could carry. Even when the distracted mother remembered a pair of child's shoes on a bedroom shelf she was not allowed to have them, a soldier's bayonet being interposed between her hands and the footwear. Mrs. Magee headed northward towards New York, a hundred miles distant, on foot. She was known to be a Royalist, and her clothing was searched for British despatches or other compromising documents. The Quakers were the only people that were kind to her and the children.

At New York City, the wives of some British officers employed her as a seamstress so that she was able to provide for herself and the two boys. The city was filled with refugees, and her son John 'picked the softer side of a plank for a bed, as I have often heard him playfully remark.'[2]

Meanwhile, Henry Magee's activities were more obscure. His great-grandchild told of an encounter with Indians, and of a white horse on which a companion was fording a river, that was shot at by Yankee marksmen. These memories must have been drawn from the time prior to 1778, when Henry reached Halifax. Whether he was part of the Nova Scotia garrison for a time, or sought civilian employment soon after his arrival, is not clear.

Mrs. Magee and the two boys remained at New York City until November 1783, when they embarked for Halifax aboard a man-of-war. Upon her arrival, someone rec-

160

*An early view of Windsor, where a village grew in the early days of Loyalist settlement. Near Windsor was Martock, the estate in the Avon River Valley on which Henry Magee worked while waiting to be reunited with his family.*

ognized her and told her that her husband was employed as a miller on the Butler estate, called 'Martock', near Windsor.

Henry Magee's wife was extremely lucky to have been recognized by other refugees from Pennsylvania and to have learned of her husband's location, for Halifax had become a town overwhelmed by Loyalist refugees, as thousands arrived there from the former British colonies to the south. A temporary tent city was set up to house some of those who could not find shelter elsewhere, while waterfront warehouses and sheds and two churches were turned into dormitories. Having heard that her husband was at 'Martock', she did not hesitate to make her way, together with the two boys, now teenagers, to Windsor on the Minas Basin.

'Martock' was a large estate in the Avon River Valley at Windsor, an important centre because it marked the end of the carriage road from Halifax as well as being a significant port. It had been founded in 1759, when a number of leading officials in Halifax had set aside large grants of land there for their families. Among the permanent residents of the area were members of the Butler family. The head of the family, John Butler, had arrived in Halifax shortly after its founding in 1749. He received a large grant of land outside Windsor on the road to Chester and named it 'Martock'. Henry Magee, as miller there, had an excellent position with good prospects for the future.

Nonetheless when he was joined by his wife and children, he decided to settle down permanently on land of his own and made his way down the Annapolis Valley to Wilmot, an area which was newly opened for settlement. When great numbers of Loyalists arrived in Halifax between September 1782 and December 1783, the provincial government worked day and night to provide for their settlement quickly and relieve the town of the huge influx of refugees. Among the arrangements was that a part of Wilmot would be set up as a separate township and named Aylesford, although for years the boundary between it and Wilmot was quite unsettled and whether a particular place was in one township or the other was often difficult to say. Henry Magee seems to have settled in this area on the King's County side close to the border

162

of Annapolis County. The land had not yet been officially granted to the Loyalist settlers when he arrived, but he received a grant in Aylesford Township in 1786.

He was "living in Wilmot" on 30 January 1786 when he appeared before the British Commissioners in Halifax to present his claim for compensation for his losses. He was part of a group of Loyalists originally from Cumberland County, Pennsylvania, who had settled in the Annapolis Valley and remained in friendly contact with each other. Henry MacGee (as his name was written by Commissioner Pemberton) served as a witness in the case of his friend Samuel Lindsay, while Samuel Lindsay and Mathew Ormsby acted as witnesses for him, attesting to his loyalty. The official record of his case states:

483. Case of HENRY MACGEE, late of Cumberland Co., Pensilvania.

Claimt. Sworn Saith:

He is a native of Ireland. He settled in America in the year 1773. When War broke out was settled in Chambers Town & then in Perth Valley in Cumberland Co. Was often asked to join the Americans, but always refused. Never signed any Association. Claimt. had a mill. When asked to grind flour for the Poor at Boston he refused. Was insulted, personally ill-treated & persecuted. Continued in this situation for 2 years, till he was taken up for Treason agst. the State, – imprisoned. He made his escape to the Mountains & joined 30 friends.

Claimant with some of his friends had formed a plan for raising a body of men to join Col. Butler, 431 had signed an agreement. The Plan miscarried from treachery of one of their own Company who turned Informer. They were obliged to disperse. Reward was offered for apprehending Claimant. He found means to get to Philadelphia & joined the British Army there. Has remained with them ever since. Was employd. afterwards in the Engineers Department at five shills, pr. Day.

Lord Cornwallis gave him 5 gs. at Philadelphia. Came to this Province in 1778, & is now settled at Wilmot.

300 acres in Westmoreland Co. The Land was purchased by Claimant of one William Delap in 1774 for £65 P. C. Claimt. had bound himself in a penalty to build a mill, which was the reason for his having it so cheap. Had not built on acct. of the times. Has no Deed. Has not heard who is now in possession of it, or what has become of it. Vals. it at 20 Shils. pr. acre.

Claimant has a Lease of a Mill in Perth Valley which he set at work & netted £100 pr. ann. by it. Had a Lease of 60 years; paid rent of 300 Bushels of grain pr. ann. Laid out £150 in setting the Mill to work.

Claimt. by Terms of his Lease was to give up the lease if he built any Mills of his own without any allowance for the expense he had been at. Claimt. had intended to build a mill of his own. Estimates his Loss at £100 pr. ann.

Produces Inventory of personal property & appraisement to amount of £135.12.9$^{1/2}$ Sterling. Swears he had all those articles & lost them & that the several articles are fairly valued.

Produces Certificates from Lieut. Asher Dunham that Claimt. was imprisoned on acct. of his Loyalty & ill used. Ow'd £51 Sterling in Pensilvania. There were Debts due to Claimant £236 Ster.

Samuel Lindsay, Wits.:

Has heard Claimt. was persecuted for his Loyalty. That he had been active in projecting an Association of Loyalists. That he was obliged to fly. Has heard he made a purchase in Westmoreland & was to build Mills there. Knew he had a Lease of Mills in Perth Valley & thinks he made a great profit by it. Knew one of the appraisers, Armstrong, who has signed the Inventory.

Mathew Ormsby, Wits.:

Lived in Pensilvania in 1774. Went to Perth Valley in 1776. Remembers the Mills which Claimt. had there. He carried on a great Trade. His house was furnished like a common good farm house.

Knew David Armstrong, one of the appraisers, & the other appraiser Getting. Armstrong was a very honest man.[3]

*An early view of Kentville, where Henry Magee settled and built a house, a watermill, and a general store, the first to serve the area.*

In the official records it is noted that Commissioner Pemberton allowed Henry Magee's claim for 136 pounds, 12 shillings, $9^{1}/_{2}$ pence. He received payment partly in money and partly in land. The Land Papers in the Archives of Nova Scotia show that on 20 September 1786 he received a grant of 500 acres (200 hectares) in Wilmot (actually in Aylesford, King's County), approximately ten kilometres east of the Annapolis County line. Later, in 1799, Henry Magee bought 600 acres (240 hectares) at Auburn about five kilometres west of Aylesford in King's County and it was there that John Magee, Henry's oldest son, built a house that has survived to the present day.

After two or three more years on his property in Aylesford, Henry Magee built a gristmill on the Kentville brook, and near it a house and a general store. There, in the tiny rural community of Horton Corner, he was once again a miller, grinding flour for nearly two more decades, 1788 to 1806. The mill and the general store were in a fine location to attract the trade which was developing in the newly settled areas as the growing population of the township of Horton spread westward along the Valley. In the earliest days of settlement by the "planters" from New England who arrived in the 1760s, Horton Town Plot, later to be named Wolfville, was the centre of commerce and social life for the settlers of the township. Within 50 years, however, Horton Corner became the larger of the two communities and eventually in 1826 became the shire town of Kentville. Although by 1800 there were only 14 houses there as well as Magee's mill and store, it grew quickly for it was a convenient place with a ford in the river at low tide; a natural place for a village.

Henry Magee's store was the first to be built in the area and was a general store which grew from the need of settlers in the district for supplies. The customers were drawn from many kilometres away, coming from the townships of Windsor, Falmouth, Horton, Cornwallis, Aylesford, and Wilmot. The store soon carried on a business amounting to over £2000 a year:

> Bishop Charles Inglis and his son Rev. John,
> Brigadier-general Morden (storekeeper of Ordnance
> at Halifax) and Colonel James Kerr of Parrsborough,

*A view of the countryside in the Annapolis Valley early in the nineteenth century. It was from such farms that many of Henry Magee's customers came to his general store for farm supplies.*

gentlemen, artisans, farmers, Indians, and slaves, all dealt with Henry Magee Sr. in his capacity as merchant, banker, pawn-broker and general facto-tum for the district.

In about 1950 when the old Magee house in Auburn, Aylesford Township, was being remodelled, the current owners found the Magee store ledgers in an attic where they had been for nearly 125 years. The old records were preserved because certain names belonging to the family, found in the records, caught the attention and interest of the finders. There were three small ledgers and four large Day Books, these last in poor condition. In total there were more than 1,100 pages, covering the years 1788 to October 1806. In the spring of 1952, Reverend Kennedy B. Wainwright, a Nova Scotian historian, was permitted to borrow and study these books. He reported his findings in 1953, using them as part of a study of the rural economy of the Annapolis Valley in the early years of its settle-ment. In his thorough analysis of the business carried out in this pioneer store, he was able to determine the wide variety of goods offered for sale by Henry Magee:

> Magee's village store dealt in everything from a needle to a plough, not to mention such items as wheat, gaspereaux, rum, snuff, and even a New Tes-tament. From an itemized list of the articles men-tioned it is almost possible to reconstruct the economy of the period – i.e. the decades immediately before and after the year 1800.[4]

The records show him to have kept careful track of his customers' accounts. If they were not paid, he turned them over to a collector, and if they were still not paid, he resorted to legal action. On 19 June 1804 he took 19 debtors to court. By such determined efforts to collect what was owed to him and by hard work and persistent effort, he was able to amass a considerable amount of gold and silver, the currency of his day. He hid the coins in unusual places which he carefully recorded in his books. There he wrote, "gold in the salt," "silver in the wheat," "gold put by in the apple box in the cellar," and "money in the loft."

*This "View of the Horton Mountains" by William Eagar, published in 1840, shows the beautiful mountain valley from which some of Henry Magee's customers were drawn.*

However, he was not entirely hard-hearted for on one occasion, which marked the only time he opened the store on a Sunday in the 18 years of its existence, he did so to provide tea, sugar, and rum for an injured man, though at a price of three shillings ten pence.

After 18 years of success in business at Horton Corner, Henry Magee died on 8 August 1806. His will was probated at Halifax by his son John Magee and two Halifax businessmen, a merchant by the name of George Grassie and a saddler, Robert Letson. The two Halifax men would not agree to act as executors of the estate, so John Magee was bonded for £8,000. He asked his brother Henry Junior and two other men to make an inventory of his father's estate. This was done and the document which was written is preserved in the Provincial Archives of Nova Scotia. It shows the comparatively large estate which Henry Magee had obtained in 20 years as a pioneer businessman:

| | |
|---|---|
| 2,000 acres of upland | £1,520 0s. 0d |
| 50 acres of improved intervale | 3,622 0. 0 |
| | |
| Immovable estate | 4,142 |
| Cash to hand this day | 41 |
| | |
| | £4,183 |

signed:  Daniel Brown
        Henry Magee
        William Bowen[5]

John Magee then took out the necessary letter of administration in King's County, papers which are on file in the Probate Office in Kentville. After her husband's death, Mrs. Magee moved to Aylesford Township to live with her son John in his house in Auburn. She lived six years longer, and was 74 years of age when she died in July 1813. Although the Magees were Methodists, there were no churches of this denomination in the area at this time and she was buried in an unmarked grave in the churchyard of St. Mary's Anglican Church in Auburn.

Henry Magee's gravestone is still clearly visible in the Oak Grove Cemetery in Kentville, a few metres from the Halifax-Annapolis highway. The upright sandstone gravestone is engraved with an inscription, still perfectly legible, which gives in a few words a summary of his life:

> In Memory of
> Henry Magee, a native
> of Ireland, an Emigrant
> from America during the
> time of the unhappy Rebel
> lion in which he was a sufferer
> and finally closed his life
> August 2. 1806 aged 67 years
> firmly attached to his King & Country
> Man that is born of a woman
> Hath but a short time to live

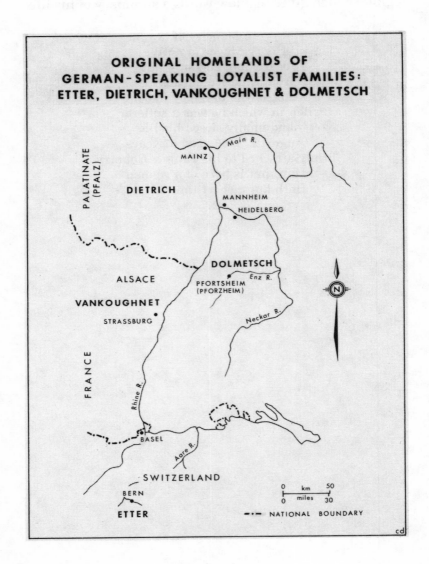

ORIGINAL HOMELANDS OF
GERMAN-SPEAKING LOYALIST FAMILIES:
ETTER, DIETRICH, VANKOUGHNET & DOLMETSCH

# Chapter Ten

# John Dulmage
# (c. 1740 – c. 1814)
# A Loyalist of Palatinate
# German Origin

*John Dulmage was a German-speaking Loyalist who was born in Courtmatrix, Ireland and died in Edwardsburgh, a Loyalist settlement in eastern Upper Canada. A Methodist in religion, he was a descendant of German Palatines who had fled from the Rhine Valley first to Holland, then to England, and eventually had settled in a planned colony of German Protestants in Ireland. As "an Irishman who spoke German" he was among the Methodist settlers of Camden Valley near Albany who took up arms as Loyalists.*

John Dulmage, Loyalist and pioneer settler in Upper Canada, was a great-grandson of Johann Adam Dolmetsch of the Lower Palatinate, believed to have been born in Pforzheim in 1678. The ancient city of Pforzheim is to the east of the Lower Rhine in an area on the edge of the Black Forest, which in 1678 was considered to be part of the Pfalz or Lower Palatinate. At that time, the Palatinate included territory on both sides of the Rhine River, although today the name is given only to lands on the west side of the river. The Dolmetsch family, with a name meaning "translator," lived in an area where soldiers of one foreign army after another passed through, leaving the countryside in ruins and the people homeless. Those who survived were taxed exorbitantly by their rulers in an effort to raise the huge sums which the wars demanded.

No one suffered more from the Thirty Years War (1618–1648) than did the farmers of the Lower Rhine. Before that event the yeomanry of Germany were in a state of great prosperity. Their homes were com-

*An engraving of a scene on the Rhine River in the Palatinate,
showing a typical village of this area, famous for its beauty.*

fortable, their barns capacious, their stables well stocked with horses and cattle, their crops were plenteous, and many had considerable sums of money safely stored away against a rainy day; some even boasted of silver plate. . . .[1]

But the events of 1709 were the most calamitous. That year, 1708–1709, was a particularly bleak one for the people of the Lower Rhine who suffered from intense cold during the winter months. They were weakened by hunger and longed for the end of the war which had lasted for six years, only the most recent in the long series of religious conflicts in the area during the past century. Each one had left the countryside and its people in more desperate circumstances. Some families from the area had accepted the invitation of William Penn to come to America where they could settle on farms of their own in a land free from religious persecution. Other families wanted to follow but lacked the means to pay their way to Pennsylvania.

In the spring of 1709 any hesitation to leave came to an end with the sudden invasion of the Palatinate by the troops of Louis XIV of France, who was determined to stamp out Protestantism. Within a matter of days in April between ten and fifteen thousand refugees fled the Lower Palatinate, making their way down the Rhine to safety in Holland. Among them were the Dolmetsches and others from the Pforzheim area.

From the countryside near Bad Durkheim came two brothers, "Henrig" and "Sabasteaen" Hack, and the latter's wife and three children. The Hacks were Lutheran and were descended from an old Danish family which had settled in Cologne 200 years earlier, eventually moving down the Rhine to the Palatinate during the course of the religious wars. A descendant of these Hacks, Sophia, was destined to become the wife of John Dulmage, Loyalist.

The Dolmetsches and the Hacks travelled in the same party of refugees as they escaped down the river. One of the Dolmetsches, Johann Adam Dolmetsch, became their leader. Also a Lutheran in religion, this man was a farmer and vinedresser, 30 years old, accompanied by his five children, although no wife is recorded. That spring the party reached Rotterdam where they joined the crowds of destitute Palatines who arrived in the Netherlands at the rate of 1,000 each week. Fortunately, "Good Queen Anne" of England offered a refuge to the Palatines, expecting that such a large number of convinced Protestants would strengthen her efforts to establish Protestantism firmly in Britain. (Actually several hundred of the refugees were Roman Catholics who were turned back if they did not agree to change their religion.) On Dutch ships commissioned by the Duke of Marlborough thousands of "Poor Palatines" crossed the channel to England. Among them was the party which included the Dolmetsches and Hacks, led by Johann Adam Dolmetsch, who was listed as heading a party of 3,000 which embarked at Rotterdam in May bound for Deptford near London.

After landing, the Palatines were sent to camps on one of the three open heaths at London – Deptford itself, Camberwell, and Blackheath. According to the records, the Hacks and the Dolmetsches were sent to the camp at Blackheath, on a low hill outside the city walls. There they awaited ships to take them to new homes. They were among the fortunate ones who were helped to settle that same summer and were not forced to camp through the winter until arrangements could be made to find homes for them in America. Instead, by the beginning of July, plans were set to place "a sturdy band with Protestant convictions" on estates owned in Ireland by English landlords. In a large party including more than 100 wagons, the women and children riding, the men on foot, they made their way by road for 350 kilometres to the port of Chester to embark on schooners for Dublin. Over 3,000 Palatines set out for permanent homes in Ireland.

After a short voyage, the Palatines arrived in Gaelic-speaking Dublin, where only the aristocracy spoke English. There they suffered from hunger in camps hurriedly put up outside the city. The Dolmetsches and Hacks were fortunate enough to be sent to the estate of Sir Thomas Southwell, a member of the Irish Parliament and a leading Protestant. He was a considerate man, fair in business dealings and kindly by nature. The Southwell estate was near Limerick, considered to be a particular stronghold of Catholicism. There, the Palatines became engaged in raising hemp and flax for the linen industry, and oats, potatoes and wheat. They soon became known for their superior farming methods: "The Palatines have benefited the country by increasing tillage, and are a laborious, independent people, who are mostly employed on their own small farms."[2] Among the most successful of these German farmers were the Dolmetsches and Hacks, or "Dulmage" and "Heck" families, as they had become known in Ireland.

During the years which followed, the Palatine settlement in Limerick flourished. The families inter-married, forming a closely knit community living in the vicinity of Courtmatrix, Ballingrane, and Killiheen, and later near Adare. Many of the Germans, among them the Dulmage family, worshipped at the Church of Ireland in Rathkeale.

In 1749, Limerick County received its first visit by the Reverend John Wesley, the English founder of Meth-odism. When three years later the first Methodist Con-ference convened in Ireland was held at Limerick City, the burgomaster of the German colony was appointed by Wesley to minister to the newly converted Palatinate Germans in Limerick County. Only a few years later, in 1760, Wesley described the three villages of Ballingrane, Courtmatrix, and Killiheen in glowing terms:

> I suppose three such towns are scarce to be found
> again in England or Ireland. There is no cursing or
> swearing, no Sabbath-breaking, no drunkedness, no
> alehouse in any of them.[3]

Among the members of the Methodist Society on the Southwell estate were the Dulmage and Heck families. One of the lay preachers of the German-speaking com-munity on the estate was a young man named Philip Embury (Imberger) who continued Wesley's work among them and won many converts for the Society.

In the spring of 1756 a small group of young people from the Southwell estate left for America. Among them was John Dulmage, the great-grandson of Johann Adam Dolmetsch, who was a young man of about 18 at the time. His mother, Margaret (Embury) Dulmage, had died when he was only nine, and two years later his father married Anna Barbara Switzer, a descendent of another Palatine immigrant of 1709, Michael Schweitzer. John Dulmage and other young people from the area had decided to emigrate mainly for economic reasons. Their Anglo-Irish landlords had been raising their rents substantially. Many tenants were afraid that they would end up deeply in debt if they did not find a solution to this problem. Emigration was seen as a solution.

However, as well as having plans to improve his economic situation in America, John Dulmage also emigrated in a spirit of adventure. Travelling with him were two particular friends, somewhat older men than he, who were professional soldiers. These were Valentine Detlor (Tetlor, or Dedler) and Detlor's friend, Edward Carscallen, a Scotch-Irish soldier. According to tradition Carscallen had been a linen weaver before entering the army. It appears that Detlor served as secretary to his father-in-law, who was commanding officer of one of the British regiments sent to America in 1756, and that it was in his capacity as secretary that he crossed the Atlantic that year. There seems to be every reason to believe that he and his two friends, John Dulmage and Edward Carscallen, went to America to engage in the French and Indian War (1755–1763).

By the summer of 1760 Paul and Barbara Heck, having recently married, also decided to leave for America. Emigration offered new opportunities and the chance for independence. Before long John Dulmage's father and two brothers and many other Germans from the Southwell estate also decided to go to America.

In their earliest years in New York City, the Dulmages and Hecks and their friends from Ireland were associated with the Lutheran Church. However, a dramatic event in 1766 brought about the founding of Methodism in America by two members of the Southwell group, Philip Embury and his cousin, Barbara Heck, the wife of John Dulmage's brother-in-law, Paul Heck, Sophia's brother.

In the second week of October, 1766, Mrs. Heck making an evening call on one of her neighbours, found them ... playing cards. Bringing her arms with a

178

sweep across the table she struck the deck of cards and dashed them into the fire, and said 'Now look at your idols; there are your gods!' From this house she proceeded to Philip Embury's house on another street.[4]

There she implored her cousin to preach again "in your own house, and to your own company." Dr. Abel Stevens has estimated the importance of the first gathering in Embury's home as follows:

Small as it was, it included white and black, bond and free, while it was also an example of that lay ministration ... which has extended the denomination in all quarters of the world, and of that agency of woman to which an inestimable proportion of the vitality and power of the Church is attributable.[5]

The small Methodist Society founded in New York City by Philip Embury soon grew into a congregation with their own chapel, a varied group of immigrants whose rousing singing of the new hymns written by Charles Wesley and the older ones by Isaac Watts attracted many new members. The work of the Methodist Society continued to flourish in New York after 1770 when Philip Embury, the Dulmages, the Hecks, and others of the German-speaking Irish group moved north to establish new homes in Camden Valley. Their ambition was to be independent and own their own farms. However, they moved into an area torn by political dissention and numerous disputes over rights and boundaries. Among their new neighbours were the Green Mountain Boys, a band of fighting farmers who warred continually against the New York land speculators, of whom the most hated was the Camden Valley settler's landlord.

From 1770 to 1773 the settlers cleared their new lands in Camden Valley, setting up a new community with Philip Embury as their burgomaster. John Dulmage was by this time in his early 30s, and had married Sophia Heck. They established their own farm in the Valley. It was "an exceedingly good farm" with "two dwelling houses and several barracks and buildings," probably indicating that there was one house for John and Sophia and their

179

family and a second one for Jacob Dulmage, John's father, and his stepmother (Anna Switzer).

From 1774 to 1776 the Dulmages and their fellow Valley settlers were caught up in the indecision and disruption caused by the growing resentment of the political and economic policies of the government in Great Britain. They were also caught between the Yankees and the Yorkers, the Green Mountain Boys and the wealthy New York landlords, who disputed land ownership in the area. In the end, their decision was to join the Loyalists. As Canadian author Eula Lapp points out:

> It is too easy to assume that their final stand was inevitable. Of course men of Palatine ancestry had special reasons to be loyal to the Crown; and Monarchs of England were, until 1837, also Electors of Hanover. However, equally persuasive forces were pulling the Valley families in the other direction. What they had finally by their labours managed to achieve, they must have yearned to retain – a community of their own; some measure of independence and of comfort; acceptance in Salem Town; and a congenial atmosphere for worship and for family life. Considering their natural conservatism and inherent dislike of violence along with their strong feelings of loyalty, and what they longed to conserve, their final decision must have been made only after much discussion and soul-searching.[6]

A number of the Palatine settlers were thrown into jail because of their support for the Crown. John Dulmage was not imprisoned, but "joined the British in '76" along with many other Camden Valley settlers. They were officially recruited by Francis Pfister. In October 1776, led by their neighbour Edward Carscallen who had recently escaped from jail, 30 Irish Palatines met with Justus Sherwood, who was leading a party towards Crown Point to join a British force there that was commanded by the Governor of Quebec, General Sir Guy Carleton. Although Sherwood was a Green Mountain Boy, the Camden Valley men agreed to join him because he knew the way better than did Edward Carscallen. In November of that year, Carleton took his regular soldiers, and several small groups of Loyalists who had joined him, north into Quebec.

That winter, John Dulmage and the other Loyalists from Camden Valley were billetted at Verchères, a picturesque village on the St. Lawrence, where they served as artificers, working on such projects as erecting barracks and repairing fortifications. By June 1777, Lieutenant-General John Burgoyne was organizing an expedition to travel along Lake Champlain and the Hudson River to Albany, where he expected to establish a firm foothold. From there, he anticipated that British troops from New York City would secure the rest of the route, thus isolating New England from the other colonies.

Burgoyne authorized the establishment of some Provincial Corps of the British Army (Loyalist regiments), among them the King's Loyal Americans under Ebenezer Jessup, the Queen's Loyal Rangers led by John Peters, and Francis Pfister's Loyal Volunteers. All those who had arrived with Justus Sherwood were placed in the Queen's Loyal Rangers, with Sherwood as their captain, and Edward Carscallen as their lieutenant. John Dulmage was one of the sergeants. Most of the Irish Palatines objected to serving under John Peters, because they had already pledged themselves to Francis Pfister. After some discussion, they agreed to serve with the Queen's Loyal Rangers for the time being.[7]

When Burgoyne's expedition left Fort St. Johns (St. Jean), southwest of Montreal, it included 3,567 British regulars, 2,919 soldiers from German states rented to George III, 148 Canadians, about 400 Indians, and an undetermined number of Provincials, perhaps 200. Along the way, more Loyalists joined the expedition, exactly how many, again, is hard to specify, but a document in the War Office records accounts for 796 Loyalists from Burgoyne's army that were known to be alive in January 1778.[8]

Most of the time, Jessup's and Peters' corps served as advance troops for the blue-coated Germans, who marched along the east side of Lake Champlain, while the red-coated British regulars marched along the west side.[9] Although the Provincials were also in red coats, they may have been put with the Germans because German-speaking men among them could communicate with these regulars. The capture of Fort Ticonderoga from the rebel army on 6 July was Burgoyne's one great success.

181

His engineers hauled two cannons up a hill overlooking the fort, which the rebels had failed to fortify. Once these guns began firing, the occupants of Ticonderoga abandoned the fort and fled southwards.

For the Irish Palatines, the most strenuous efforts were made on 16 August, at the Battle of Bennington, when 500 Loyalists of Peters' and Pfister's corps accompanied 1,000 German regulars on a foraging expedition to capture supplies. Most of Peters' men were placed at the rear, but Sherwood's company and Pfister's men occupied a redoubt in the forward position – perhaps to appease those in Sherwood's company who had wanted to join Pfister in the first place. Burgoyne reported that 1,220 men were lost at Bennington. Pfister was among the dead. Of Sherwood's company, 60 strong at the outset, 46 survived, but John Dulmage was missing. Dulmage was, however, only lost in the confusion and he arrived a day or so later at Burgoyne's camp on the Hudson River.[10]

Although Sherwood had had fewer casualties than most of the other companies, on 22 August, led by Lieutenant Edward Carscallen, 25 men, including Paul Heck and John's own brother, David Dulmage, asked to leave Peters' corps to serve under Captain Samuel McKay, who had taken command of the dead Pfister's corps. Burgoyne permitted the transfer, to Sherwood's dismay, but one Irish Palatine who did not leave him was Sergeant John Dulmage. His motives were not stated, but John may have felt that Sherwood would be at a disadvantage if he had to continue serving with the German troops without the aid of an interpreter. From that day, a firm bond of affection and respect was forged between the Yankee and the Irish Palatine. Sherwood asked that Dulmage be promoted to lieutenant, to replace Carscallen, to which Burgoyne agreed.[11]

By September, Burgoyne's demoralized regular troops were in desperate need of reinforcements. John Dulmage was among 120 men "of tried bravery, and Fidelity from the Provincial Corps" who were incorporated into six British regiments, 20 added to each. He, like the others, was to receive a special gratuity on joining his regiment, and another on leaving it "on the following Christmas day." In the battle near Saratoga which took place on 7

October, Burgoyne and his men were defeated and suffered heavy losses.

Ten days later, the Saratoga Convention was signed and Burgoyne soon returned to England, a failure. By the terms of the Convention, Burgoyne's men were to surrender their arms, and as prisoners of war were to march to Boston and then return home by sea with the understanding that they would not fight again. However, John Dulmage and other Provincials did not have the same status as the other prisoners of war, and Burgoyne feared for their safety. Consequently, they were released from duty the night before the surrender. With permission, several hundred left the camp and escaped northwards through Vermont to Canada. Among them were John Dulmage and several other men from Camden Valley.

Back in Canada the Provincials lived in groups under officers responsible to Sir John Johnson, quartered in Sorel, Montreal, and Quebec. Some of the men from Camden Valley were quartered at Verchères again, others at Châteauguay nearby. Sometime in 1778, the Dulmage farm was confiscated, and John's wife, Sophia, and his seven children – Philip, Samuel, Jacob, Margaret, Elisabeth, Elias and Ann – arrived in Quebec. With several other Valley families, they had travelled from Albany County to St. Johns and on to join husband and father. Like the other refugee women, Sophia could only take with her what belongings the family could carry, which included provisions for only two weeks.

In June 1781, Captain Justus Sherwood was placed in command of the British Secret Service, Northern Department, by the then governor, General Frederick Haldimand. Sherwood's headquarters were in a new blockhouse on North Hero Island in Lake Champlain, a secluded place for the arrival and departure of "secret scouts." Lieutenant John Dulmage took command of the blockhouse garrison, responsible for day to day administration of the post, but he was not a party to the more secret intrigues, which Sherwood kept to himself.[12]

That November, the remnants of Burgoyne's Provincials, and some fresh recruits, were amalgamated to form a new regiment, the Loyal Rangers. Sherwood re-

*James Peachey, the artist of this view of Cataraqui (Kingston) in 1783, was a member of Samuel Holland's survey party which camped in tents near the ruins of the French Fort Frontenac while they laid out the land nearby for Loyalist settlement. In the foreground are either local Mississauga Indians or possibly a party of Mohawks looking for areas suitable for Mohawk settlement.*

ceived a company, some of whom did duty at his block-house, and a new lieutenant, James Parrot to supervise them, for Dulmage was fully occupied with his other duties. In a list headed "Officers' names, Characters and Pretensions" next to his name are the words: "an active intelligent man, very fit for laborious service." Elsewhere, Sherwood described him as "a very good, careful Man. . . ."[13]

On 24 December 1783, the Loyal Rangers were disbanded, and plans were already under way for their re-settlement. Between June and August 1784, the majority travelled by bateaux from temporary encampments along the lower St. Lawrence to permanent homes in the west.

While the Heck family stayed in Montreal, the Dulmages were among those who moved west in 1784. John Dulmage settled with his family in Edwardsburgh Township, near the site of what is now Prescott. Ultimately, his lieutenant's commission entitled him to 2,000 acres (800 hectares). The first grant he received was Lot 35 and the west half of Lot 34 in the first concession of the township. His brother David, meanwhile, settled in the Fifth Town (Marysburgh Township) in present-day Prince Edward County. In 1785, Paul and Barbara Heck (who in 1766 had been instrumental in founding the Methodist Society in America) settled in Augusta Township, the first one west of Edwardsburgh. Although many of the Palatines from Camden Valley lived in Lower Canada at first, eventually all but one, Peter Miller, moved to Upper Canada. They settled in one of two places, either at New Oswegatchie (the name given to the townships occupied by Loyal Rangers, approximately the sites of Prescott and Brockville) or along the Bay of Quinte.

There in these two settlements in the eastern part of Upper Canada the "German-speaking Irish" from Camden Valley soon succeeded in establishing Methodism. They made contact with other members of their faith in the state of New York, where the movement was becoming fairly established and progressing rapidly. The first itinerant Methodist preachers from the United States soon arrived in their midst. In 1786 George Neal crossed the Niagara River and preached at Queenston, while four years later the first preacher arrived in the Bay of Quinte

*A nineteenth century sketch of the Old "Blue" Church, near modern Prescott, Ontario. In the cemetery may be seen the grave of Barbara Heck, who died on 17 August 1804.*

*Hay Bay Church, the first Methodist Chapel in Upper Canada, erected in 1792.*

area. These "circuit riders" who brought Methodism to the isolated and struggling pioneers were welcomed by the Palatines, as has been recorded in Methodist Church history:

> The first regular Methodist itinerant who came to Canada was William Losee, who, in January, 1790, came to see some of his U.E. Loyalist relatives and friends, who had settled in Adolphustown. He had preached his way from Lake Champlain Circuit to Canada, and along through Matilda, Augusta, Elizabethtown and Kingston, and then throughout the Bay of Quinte townships, until a flame of revival was kindled and many converted. . . . The first [organized] class in Canada was formed on the Hay Bay shore, Sunday, February 20th, 1791. . . . The first Methodist chapel was built on Paul Hough's lot, Hay Bay. . . . There had been a class formed in Augusta as early as 1788, made up of Paul and Barbara Heck, their three sons, some of the Emburys, and perhaps other Methodists who, influenced by feelings of loyalty to the British crown, had left New York. . . . The Irish Palatines, who bore the 'precious seed' across the sea and became the founders of Methodism in New York, were thus the founders also of Methodism in Canada.[14]

When William Losee arrived in Canada he reported that in Augusta he found "a people prepared for the Lord," and mentioned by name three of the Palatine families, the Hecks, the Lawrences, and the Dulmages. By the time their lives ended, nearly 30 years after their arrival in Quebec, John and Sophia Dulmage had seen the firm establishment of Methodism in Upper Canada. Sophia died in 1810, and her son-in-law, Reverend Samuel Coate (her daughter Ann's husband) recounted:

> . . . my father-in-law went down upon his knees to commend her soul into the hands of God. He expressed all the tenderness of a kind husband, and . . . all the resignation of a Christian . . . [15]

John Dulmage lived at least until 1813, possibly somewhat longer, leaving behind him a large family of devout Methodists. A man of deep religious convictions, John Dulmage had been a brave, dutiful soldier, and later a major, in the Upper Canadian Militia. His sons served in the militia, and in November 1838, his grandson and namesake, Lieutenant John Dulmage, was killed in action at the Battle of the Windmill, when a band of Americans and Canadian rebels attempted to raid Prescott.

*This watercolour painting by James Peachey is a view of Niagara near where a number of members of Butler's Rangers settled after 1784, among them James Dittrick. His family is said to be the first to live where present day St. Catharines now stands.*

# Chapter Eleven

# Jacob Dittrick
# (1755–1828)
# A First Settler at St. Catharines

By John S. Dietrich, Q.C.

*One of the sergeants in Butler's Rangers was Jacob Dittrick, a man in his early 20s who had left the Mohawk Valley of New York to make his way to Niagara, where the Loyalist force under Colonel John Butler made its headquarters. Following the revolution he settled with his family and other members of Butler's Rangers in the Niagara Peninsula, in his case the banks of Twelve Mile Creek on the site of present-day St. Catharines. The Dittricks, and many of their friends and relatives, were descendants of Palatine Germans who had settled in the Mohawk Valley some 70 years earlier.*

The name Dittrick was spelled in many ways, such as Dedrick, Tedrick, Fredrick, Frederick. All were variations of the original name, Dietrich, still a common surname and Christian name in German-speaking areas of Europe. The Dietrichs, like other Palatines, were victims of war that devastated their farmlands along the banks of the Rhine River or in the nearby countryside, an area known as the Lower Palatinate, or Pfalz. The Palatinate suffered cruelly at the hands of Louis XIV's army, when in 1709 the French King decided to make the area useless for his enemies, and to punish the inhabitants for giving shelter to Protestant refugees from his neighbouring French provinces, such as Alsace. When Louis' army overran the Rhine Valley of the Palatinate, between ten and fifteen thousand people fled to Rotterdam and crossed the Channel as refugees, on the invitation of Queen Anne.[1]

Some were resettled in Ireland, while many went on to find new homes and religious tolerance in the Queen's overseas colonies. Included in this Palatine migration were Protestants from other European countries, such as Scandinavia, the Netherlands, as well as France, and from other German-speaking areas. Some came from Moravia, in the west, while some were Mennonites from Switzerland. The opportunity to move to the British Isles or to America meant that for the first time in 100 years of strife, they could have the right to worship God according to the religion of their choice. At the time of the American Revolution, many people of Palatine descent had not forgotten the gratitude of their families for the safe haven England's Queen Anne had offered them, and they refused to side with the American rebels, who were styling themselves "Patriots."

In 1775, when people were beginning to choose sides, Jacob Dittrick, grandson of one of the Palatines who reached America in 1710, was living on a farm in New York's Mohawk Valley near the site of Utica. Most of the Palatines there chose to support the King, for past assistance. They had fared well under British rule and were suspicious of the rebels and their talk of independence. Yet some Palatines did side with the rebels, some out of fear and resentment. Sir William Johnson, the largest landowner in the Mohawk Valley, had imported Gaelic-speaking Roman Catholics from the Scottish Highlands to populate his estates and to help relieve the suffering caused by the Jacobite uprising of 1745-46. Sir William's son and heir, Sir John Johnson, was a Loyalist, and his Highland tenants followed his lead. However, despite their fear of their Roman Catholic neighbours, most of the Palatines made common cause. Among them was Jacob Dittrick, who elected to serve under another Mohawk Valley landlord, John Butler.

Service in any Loyalist regiment – or Provincial Corps of the British Army, the proper title – was rigorous. Service with Butler's Rangers was beyond a doubt the most demanding of all. Although a muster roll for each Provincial Corps was supposed to be filed with the War Office, none has been found for Butler's Rangers. Lieutenant-Colonel William A. Smy, of the Lincoln and Welland Regiment, has compiled a list of the men who served in the corps, which he admits is not complete, showing nearly

900 men *known* to have served in Butler's Rangers (the ancestor of his own regiment). Since full strength for the rangers was 500, this shows a much higher rate of attrition than for most of the Provincial Corps of the American Revolutionary era. Jacob Dittrick was a ranger from at least June 1777 until the corps was disbanded in 1784. That he survived to resettle and raise a large family is a tribute to his rugged constitution.

Jacob's date of birth was 1755; therefore he was serving with the rangers at age 22. No claim for compensation has been found, a hint that he went from his father's farm and had no property of his own. However, his son James, writing in 1860, said that his father had inherited the farm in the Mohawk Valley before he enlisted with the rangers.[2] Also, according to family tradition, Jacob Dittrick was well acquainted with John Butler, the commander of the corps, before the war. Butler's large estate, called Butlersbury, at Fonda, in the Mohawk Valley, was confiscated by the rebels.

Butler had long been a colonel in the New York Militia, as well as an agent in the Indian Department. In July 1775, John Butler and other officers of the Indian Department and many followers, joined Guy Johnson, the Superintendent of Indian Affairs, and travelled to Oswego, on Lake Ontario. All felt threatened by the local rebels, whose plan to have Guy Johnson kidnapped had been revealed to them by friendly natives. From Oswego they descended the St. Lawrence River to Montreal. Since Guy Johnson went to England on a leave of absence, the governor of Canada, Guy Carleton, appointed John Butler a deputy in the Indian Department and sent him to Fort Niagara, the departmental headquarters.[3] Jacob Dittrick could have been among Butler's followers in Montreal, or else he left his farm for Fort Niagara at a later date.

The first record of Jacob's presence at Fort Niagara is his name – shown as Jacob Frederick – on "A List of Persons Employed as Rangers in the Indian Department" dated 15 June 1777.[4] He was being paid four shillings New York currency per day, slightly more than two shillings Sterling, and the rate which Butler allowed men who spoke Indian languages. This evidence supports the contention of James Dittrick, Jacob's son, that his father was well liked by the aboriginal peoples of the Mohawk Valley.

In June 1777, John Butler did not have permission to raise a regiment. His only orders from Governor Carleton were to raise a large body of Indians to help in a major thrust by British and Provincial troops from Canada. The main force, led by Lieutenant-General John Burgoyne, was to proceed from Montreal by Lake Champlain and the Hudson River to Albany. A smaller expedition under Colonel Barry St. Leger, a British regular officer, was to assemble at Oswego and proceed through the Mohawk Valley to meet Burgoyne and his army at Albany. To this latter force Carleton assigned Butler and the Indians. Butler went a step farther, by signing up 67 Loyalists as rangers on 15 June, and putting them on the payroll of the Indian Department.

Neither expedition reached Albany. Burgoyne surrendered his army at Saratoga on 17 October. St. Leger's force was stalled outside Fort Stanwix (the site of Rome, New York) early in August, for he lacked guns heavy enough to reduce the rebel-held fort. While St. Leger's force was investing the fort, he learned that a rebel relief column was marching west to relieve Stanwix, and he ordered Sir John Johnson, with his fledgling King's Royal Regiment of New York, then numbering 133 men, Butler and his rangers, and the Mohawk war chief, Joseph Brant, leader of the native warriors, to set up an ambush in a gorge at Oriskany, ten kilometres east of the fort. What followed, on 6 August 1777, was one of the bloodiest battles of the revolution.

All the contestants were Mohawk Valley men, brother against brother, father against son. Both sides claimed a victory, Johnson, Butler and Brant because they dispersed the rebel column, the rebels because St. Leger proceeded no farther. Instead he withdrew to Oswego to await the arrival of heavier guns which he had ordered sent from Fort Niagara. At Oswego, St. Leger received orders from Burgoyne to bring his regulars and Sir John Johnson's men and reinforce his main army on the Hudson River, which was then in difficulty.[5] St. Leger and Sir John left for Montreal, and Butler took his rangers back to Fort Niagara. Unless he was ill or unfit for service, Jacob Dittrick, at age 22, was a veteran of the Battle of Oriskany.

In September, Butler went to Quebec City and received a warrant from Governor Carleton to raise his regiment of rangers. Two companies were to "serve with the Indians, as occasion shall require," the men to be paid four shillings New York per day. Men in the other companies were to be paid two shillings New York per day. This was twice as much as privates serving in regular regiments or other Provincial Corps received, but Butler insisted, knowing that if his men were captured they would be treated as traitors and he needed the extra inducement. At the same time the inducement was slight. Men in other corps were clothed and equipt, but rangers were expected to provide their own firearms and pay towards their clothing.[6]

Jacob Dittrick was appointed a sergeant in one of the companies of men conversant in Indian languages, and he received higher pay than the privates, but the amount was not specified in Butler's warrant. For the next six years Jacob fought a guerrilla war whose main purposes were to destroy the rebels' food supply, to gather intelligence, and to support the native peoples. The latter were battling settlers encroaching on their lands in defiance of Britain's policy of reserving the territory west of the Allegheny Mountains for the various tribes.

The rangers did indeed range – from their main base at Fort Niagara as far east as New Jersey, across northern New York and in Pennsylvania. Detachments based at Detroit supported the natives as far south as the Kentucky Valley, where, in August 1782, they defeated the American frontier folk hero, Daniel Boone, at the Battle of Blue Licks.

Jacob Dittrick could have been a scout at times, part of a large expedition at others, or possibly the leader of a small party of rangers who joined Indian warriors under the direction of an officer of the Indian Department. Rangers travelled light, carrying few provisions and for the most part living off the country. They received food from Loyalists still in their homes, from Indians, or they took what livestock and food they needed from rebel supporters on whom they preyed. They did without blankets, and often slept in the woods in bitter cold, not daring to light fires since smoke would betray their presence. Often they lived on a few ears of green corn, or horsemeat, and they marched through snow in shoes or moccasins worn to shreds. They returned to Niagara or Detroit mere wraiths, clothes in tatters and almost barefoot.[7]

All this hardship Jacob Dittrick survived, although his name was never mentioned in the regiment's records. Sergeants rarely were, unless they did something spectacularly good, or spectacularly bad, such as desert, attack a woman, steal, or start a fight in the barracks. Jacob was a moral man, as his later life showed, and apparently his missions were not the stuff of which heros are made.

Despite all the raiding and scouting, Jacob found time to fall in love. In 1777, William Pickard, from Westmoreland County in Pennsylvania, brought his family to Fort Niagara. As the name suggests, he was of French Huguenot descent. William enlisted in the rangers, and so did two of his sons, Benjamin and James, one as a private, the other as a drummer.[8] William Pickard's daughter Margaret was 15 when she came to Fort Niagara, and she soon caught the fancy of Jacob Dittrick. At some point they were married. While the men were away campaigning, Margaret and her mother lived in a cabin at Four Mile Creek, as the name suggests, four miles south of Fort Niagara on the New York side of the Niagara River, where other Loyalists driven from their homes were encamped. There, on 9 October 1780, Catherine, the first Dittrick child was born. She may have been named after John Butler's wife, Catharine. This daughter was followed on 20 January 1783 by a son Robert, thought to have been named after the regimental surgeon, Robert Guthrie.[9] Palatines made a practice of naming their children after people they respected.

The regiment was disbanded in June 1784, and Jacob moved his family to the Ontario side of the Niagara River, to land owned by "Captain MacDonald" (possibly Captain John MacDonell of the rangers).[10] There, on 29 August 1785, their second son, James, was born. Family tradition says that James was named after James Secord, for a time a lieutenant in the rangers but later the tavern keeper at Fort Niagara. Secord, a much older man than

*The sons and daughters of Loyalists were granted land when they came of age, or earlier in the case of a daughter who married before the age of 21. When they took up their land, usually in an area just opening up for settlement, they had to clear it and improve the property to make a livable pioneer home and farm such as the one illustrated here.*

Jacob, had found life as a ranger officer too strenuous. When land grants were given out, Jacob received 400 acres (160 hectares) at Twelve Mile Creek, now the site of St. Catharines, for his services as a sergeant. Thus he was one of the first settlers in that part of the Niagara Peninsula.

A man of deep religious convictions rooted in his Palatine forebears, Jacob was one of the subscribers to the first church erected at the "Twelve" as the people styled their settlement at first. He was also one of the largest contributors, promising to donate, on a list dated 17 February 1796, the sum of twenty-six pounds, ten shillings and sixpence New York money.[11] The church was an Anglican one, and probably not Jacob's original denomination, but under Governor John Graves Simcoe it was also intended as the established one. By 1819, Jacob was shown as one of the church's trustees, appealing to Jacob Mountain, the Anglican Bishop of Quebec, for "a pious clergyman, we paying him 50 pounds currency per year, and provide him with a respectable parsonage house &c." At first, services had been conducted in the settlement only occasionally, by the first Anglican clergyman in the Niagara area, the Reverend Robert Addison.

During the War of 1812, the church served as a hospital for wounded soldiers, and the women of the community nursed them and brought them nourishing food. By that time, the former Sergeant Jacob Dittrick had become a major in the militia and was on active service. He was also the father of a large family.

On Jacob's farm at the "Twelve" were born, Margaret on 4 October 1788, Jacob Junior, 12 February 1791, Walter, 31 May 1793, William, 20 December 1795, Jamima, 12 March 1799, George, 20 December 1801, Rebecca, 23 October 1803, and Caroline, 20 November 1807. Their names were recorded in the Dittrick family Bible, which has been preserved. At age 21, or in the case of a daughter, earlier if she married before that age, as children of a U.E. Loyalist, each of the Dittricks' offspring was eligible for a grant of 200 acres (80 hectares), a regulation that had been passed by an order-in-council in 1789. Some received land not far from St. Catharines, but two of Jacob's sons, Walter and William, received theirs in Lanark County near

Packenham, a pretty village 50 kilometres west of Ottawa. Given the conditions of travel at the time, this was a very long way from home.[12]

William added a new dimension to the family's ethnic mix, for he chose as his wife a Miss Thornton of Perth. Her father had been an officer in Wellington's army in Spain, where he had married a Spanish woman. After his discharge in England, the Thorntons settled on a farm near Perth, a town founded by veterans of the Napoleonic Wars. Jacob Dittrick's son William changed his name to Dietrich, the correct German spelling, which has been used ever since by his branch of the family.

William's son, John Dietrich, operated a steamboat on the Tay Canal, which linked Perth to the Rideau Waterway before the arrival of the Canadian Pacific Railway Line to the town. John also sold and erected most of the windmills used to pump water on local farms, and the remains of some of these mills are still standing today. He established a bolt factory and a foundry for the manufacture of farm implements, and he also sold the first automobiles in the Perth area. In.1866 he served in the militia during the Fenian Raids, when citizen soldiers garrisoned Fort Wellington at Prescott, a railway wheelhouse on the Brockville waterfront, and guarded the canals at Cornwall.

The Dietrichs, and many other families of Loyalist origin, spread through the nation as generation succeeded generation, so that descendants are to be found all over the country, and in many parts of the United States. Many descendants are unaware that their Loyalist ancestor was Jacob Dittrick. However, one branch of the family tree has been documented to the present — those in the William Dietrich line that spread its branches from Perth. Fortunately, as interest in genealogy grows, many more people will discover a connection to Jacob Dittrick, just as other families are uncovering the multicultural nature of their roots, and those of so many of Ontario's founders.

*Portrait of Sa Ga Yeath Qua Pieth Tow (called Brant), 1710, by John Verelst. Brant was one of the four chieftains who visited the court of Queen Anne of England, and was instrumental in settling the homeless Palatines in new homes in the Mohawk Valley.*

# Chapter Twelve

# Jacob Johnson (Tekahionwake) (b. circa 1760) A Mohawk and Loyalist

*Baptized Jacob Johnson, this Loyalist always used his Mohawk name, Tekahionwake ("double wampum"). Orphaned in his youth, the young Mohawk was put in the care of Sir William Johnson, the British colonial leader charged with maintaining good relations with the Mohawks in the Albany region before the American Revolution, when the Six Nations Indians occupied territory along the Mohawk River. When the Six Nations moved to Upper Canada as Loyalists and settled along the Grand River, Jacob Johnson and his sister joined them there. Jacob's son, Sakayengwaraton, also known as Chief John "Smoke" Johnson, distinguished himself in the War of 1812 and became one of the greatest leaders of the Mohawks of the nineteenth century. John was the grandfather of the gifted Mohawk poet Pauline Johnson, one of the best known of early Canadian writers.*

According to tradition, the league of tribes which later became known as the Six Nations was founded at some period in the fifteenth century when five tribes – Mohawk, Oneida, Onondaga, Cayuga, and Seneca – bound themselves together with the aim of securing a lasting peace. In the early eighteenth century, the Tuscaroras were admitted to the League, so that it included six nations. "The Confederacy of the Six Nations of the Longhouse," or the Iroquois, as the French named them, was a powerful confederation of tribes which supported the British cause in the wars fought against the French and their Indian supporters in the early years of the British colonization of America.

The Indians of the Confederacy of Six Nations were proud and honest, known for their bravery in battle. Their

*"King" Hendrik (Thoyanoguen or Theyanoguin) succeeded Brant as the leader of the Mohawks, and maintained the friendship with the British established by his predecessor.*

system of government was complex and sophisticated, and extremely efficient. It bound them into a closely-knit group living under strict rules of order. Women had great power, older ones acting as advisers in tribal councils. Children belonged to their mother's clan, one of several, each of which had a special totem such as a bear, tortoise or wolf. A man could not marry into his own particular clan, but could marry into a more distant tribe if he so wished. War chiefs were usually selected by the leaders of the tribe, sometimes by the women.

The Mohawks settled in the valley of the Mohawk River in what is now northern New York State, in a strategic location where the river serves as a link between Lake Ontario, by way of rivers and lakes, to Lake Champlain and the Richelieu and St. Lawrence rivers. The river valley is fertile and quiet, with low flats along the winding banks and wooded hills on each side. By the eighteenth century, the Mohawks were both farmers and traders having built wooden houses and planted crops in the Mohawk Valley. They also acted as middlemen in the profitable fur-trade between the British and the Indians of the western regions.

In 1710 one of the officers in charge of maintaining good relations with the Indians of the Albany area, Colonel Peter Schuyler, took four of the elders or "sachems" of the Six Nations to visit the court of Queen Anne in London.[1] There they were greeted as visiting kings and treated with great honour. Their portraits were painted by court artists. These paintings show four finely dressed Indian aristocrats in formal pose representing their nations at the royal court. As part of their entertainment they were given a tour of London, then crowded with thousands of homeless Palatines who had fled from the devastation of their land along the Rhine. The Indian sachems were shocked by the plight of these German-speaking Protestant refugees. One of them, Brant or Sagayean Qua Tra Ton, a leader of the Mohawks and grandfather of Joseph Brant, invited the Palatines to settle on his lands along the Mohawk River. This generous offer to share his lands brought many of the penniless refugees to the Mohawk Valley, where they settled in the area later called German Flats, and from there spread out into other parts of the valley and into Pennsylvania.

Brant and his family lived at Canajoharie, a name which means "a pot that washes itself clean" and refers to the bed of a fast flowing creek nearby. There they lived in a settlement of wooden houses, near fields where they grew corn and other crops. Following the death of Brant, Hendrik (Theyanoguin) succeeded as sachem. He continued the policy of giving the full support of the Mohawks to the British government. Many of the Mohawks had become Christians, converted by the missionaries of the Anglican church. Evelyn H.C. Johnson, a descendant of Jacob Johnson has described this early missionary work in the following way:

> The early missionaries made Niagara their place of appointment for meetings with the Indians, and as travel through the forest as well as by water was slow and difficult, the missionaries were accustomed to periodically visit certain sections of the country to instruct the Indians in the Christian religion, baptize the children, and hold services in the forests for the benefit of the people. As all of the Indians knew the Falls of Niagara, it is but natural that Niagara became the leading place for these gatherings.[2]

At one of these religious gatherings in the 1760s at Niagara Falls in New York State, Jacob Johnson's parents presented him for baptism. It was an unusually important meeting that year, for Sir William Johnson, the British Superintendent of Indian Affairs, Northern District, was present on the occasion. He was attending in honour of some of his Mohawk friends who had come to join in the ceremonies. Tekahionwake and his wife had called their infant son Jacob, but wanted to select a second name. According to one of Jacob's descendants, Sir William offered his own name to the child:

> There was some delay over the decision of a second name for the child, and learning the cause, their Superintendent-General, Sir William Johnson, came forward and said, 'Name him Johnson after me.' This was immediately done, and the boy was baptized Jacob Johnson.[3]

*An engraving by Charles Mottram entitled "Lake Superior, Showing Voyages on the Lake" illustrates the mode of travel of Indians and fur traders who brought furs from the western tribes to the east of Canada.*

Another explanation of the name by still another descendant is that Sir William Johnson was the godfather of the child, who was not a baby but a young boy at the time.

Another family tradition, supported by many members of the Johnson family, is the story of Jacob's travels as a youth. It appears that Jacob and his two-year-older sister Mary lost their father when they were quite young. Their widowed mother married a Wyandotte, and moved to a distant area along with her new husband, taking the two children with her. It is believed that they travelled into the area now known as Kansas where some of the Wyandottes had gone on a long migration. The mother died not long after the journey was over and the children were left alone and without friends in a part of the country unfamiliar to them. The Wyandottes sent word to the Mohawks asking that the children be sent for.

The council of the Six Nations sent a representative of the family to accompany the children back to the Mohawk Valley. It was a woman, a distant relative, who offered to make the long journey. She travelled by horse alone through the wilderness for a great distance before reaching the Wyandotte's country where she was able to locate the two children. With even greater difficulty, she brought the children back on her horse:

> She set out with the two children on horseback; one sat in front and one behind her. When she reached the river she had crossed on her way to the Wyandots' Country, she left one of the children on the bank, and taking the other with her she made her horse swim the river as before. Leaving this child on the opposite shore she returned for the other one, and thus brought them safely across the river, and continuing her journey finally reached her home and people in the Mohawk Valley.[4]

After their return, the two orphans were in the care of the Six Nations. It appears that Sir William Johnson, perhaps in his capacity as godfather of the children, asked the Mohawk leader Joseph Brant to assume responsibility for their welfare. Brant agreed, and eventually sent

*Joseph Brant was instrumental in having the Old Mohawk Church built on the lands settled by the Six Nations near present day Brantford. This engraving shows the chapel as it appeared 100 years ago at the time of the centennial of the arrival of the Loyalists.*

them to Sandusky, Ohio, in the care of two Indians. There they remained for several years while the American Revolution was in progress. After the war was over, the Mohawks, as Loyalists, were forced to abandon their homes in the Mohawk Valley. Led by Joseph Brant, some of the Mohawks settled in the area laid out for them along the banks of the Grand River. Soon, Brant sent for the two young Mohawk orphans in Sandusky, Ohio. Mary, then about 20, and Jacob, 18, travelled from the Ohio to the Grand River settlement, where Jacob was destined to be the founder of a famous family.

Jacob Johnson, or as he was always known, Tekahionwake, married twice. The name of his first wife is not known, but his second wife was nicknamed Chee-toh-leh. It was the first wife who was the mother of Jacob's distinguished son, John Johnson, or Sakayengwaraton, the first of the family to use the English name Johnson. He was usually known as Smoke Johnson. The nickname "Smoke" was taken from his Mohawk name which had the meaning "the early morning mist of Indian Summer" or "he has made the mist disappear for them." Mist is known as "smoke" to the Mohawks, so the nickname became attached to John Johnson. He grew up on the Brantford reserve as a full-blooded Mohawk, a member of the bear clan. Like his father before him, he was an Anglican and a member of the Mohawk Church which had been built for the Indians in 1785, soon after their arrival as Loyalists.

As a young man, Smoke Johnson fought in the War of 1812 in battles at Queenston Heights, Beaver Dams, Lundy's Lane, and Stoney Creek. According to tradition, he was the soldier who set the fire which devastated Buffalo in 1813. After the war he was awarded a pension for his services. In 1815, on his return home, he married Helen Martin, the daughter of an important Mohawk chieftain, George Martin, one of the Loyalists who had settled on the Grand River.

Helen Martin's mother was Catherine Rolleston, a white woman. About the year 1774, the Mohawks attacked white settlers in Pennsylvania as a revenge for the treatment given to Chief Logan, whose family had been massacred. While searching the houses of the Dutch and

German settlers, the Mohawks found a house in which a Dutch girl of about 13 years of age had been left behind when the family fled. She was captured and adopted by one of the important chiefs of the Confederacy, and eventually learned the Mohawk language and customs. Her adopted father, Teyonhahwekea, and his family were given the task of assuring the safety of the great treasures, the Peace Pipe and the Queen Anne Silver. For some time, these were buried, some say at Niagara where the Mohawks stayed for a time, others say in the Mohawk Valley. In any case, a party was sent to retrieve the treasures. According to the Martin family tradition, it was Catherine Rolleston who solved the problem of bringing them back safely:

> Taking some old clothing and a quantity of rags, she wrapped therein the Peace Pipe and the treasured communion service, together with the wealth of silver brooches which belonged to her family. This she made into a bundle, in appearance – only a bundle of rags. Placing this on her back she adjusted the Indian carrying belt across her forehead and was ready for the trail.
>
> Catherine and her companions were accompanied by soldiers who constantly urged them on. The story goes that a soldier, urging her forward, thrust his bayonet into the bundle on her back. The point of it must have struck one of the plates, for to this day it bears the mark. After its safe arrival it was divided, part being retained by the Grand River Mohawks and part being held by the Mohawks of the Bay of Quinte. The marked piece is at the Bay of Quinte Reserve.[5]

Smoke Johnson and Helen Martin had a large family. According to Mohawk custom they lived with Helen's parents at Bow Park near Brantford until the first child was born. Then they moved to their own farm about three kilometres to the north of the Martin homestead.

As a young man, Smoke Johnson was well acquainted with the Mohawk leader, Joseph Brant. They both attended the Mohawk Chapel, still standing in Brantford. Both took part in the Indian dancing which

*John Smoke Johnson is seen standing, third from the left, in this group photograph of Indian chiefs taken by the Electric Studio of Brantford. Left to right are Joseph Snow, Onondaga Chief; George Henry Martin Johnson, the father of Pauline Johnson, Mohawk; John Buck, Onondaga; John Smoke Johnson, Mohawk, father of George Henry Martin Johnson; Isaac Hill, Onondaga; John Seneca Johnson, Seneca.*

served as entertainment for visitors to the settlement. This dancing has been described by Patrick Campbell, who visited Joseph Brant in 1792, when the settlement on the Grand River had only been established for a few years:

> After dinner Captain Brant, that he might not be wanting in doing me the honours of his nation, directed all the young warriors to assemble in a certain large house, to show me the war dance, to which we all adjourned about nightfall. Such as were at home of the Indians appeared superbly dressed in their most showy apparal, glittering with silver, in all the variety, shapes, and forms of their fancies, which made a dazzling appearance; the pipe of peace with long white feathers, and that of war with red feathers, equally long, were exhibited in their first war dance, with shouts and war hoops resounding to the skies. The chief himself held the drum, beat time, and often joined in the song, with a certain cadence to which they kept time. The variety of forms into which they put their bodies, and agility with which they changed from one strange posture to another, was really curious to an European eye not accustomed to such a sight.[6]

On one occasion, some years later, Smoke Johnson was one of the young warriors who travelled with Joseph Brant to Montreal and danced for the entertainment of the others in his party and for guests.

Smoke Johnson was known for his great gift as an orator, both in English and Mohawk, for he was equally familiar with both languages. This ability soon made him a highly valued assistant to the British superintendent of the Six Nation Indians. On the recommendation of the Indian Department he was made a chief, and for over 40 years he served as speaker of the Grand River Council. He was so eloquent that he became known as The Mohawk Warbler, a title of honour in a period when oratory was much appreciated, both by the Mohawks and their neighbours in the growing community of Brantford. One of his last speeches was given in 1886 when the cornerstone was laid for the Brantford monument to Joseph Brant and the

Indians of the Six Nations. His address was reported as follows:

> Chief John Smoke Johnson (grandfather of Pauline Johnson) ninety-four years old, who was through the war of 1812-15, gave an address in a voice remarkable for its clearness. He had known Brant very well and had also heard of the works he had done in times of war. When the Mohawks lived in New York State with great privileges and advantages the revolution had suddenly broken out. Brant immediately allied himself with the British troops and when after continuous fighting the British were forced to retire, Brant and his warriors guided the British soldiers safely from the Mohawk river to Niagara, and then returned and brought their wives and children also safely to them.[7]

Smoke Johnson's eldest son also served as a Six Nations chief and interpreter. He was George Henry Martin Johnson, or Onwanonsyshon, who was born in 1816 and died two years before his father in 1884. He received a good education at the Mohawk Institute, the school established for the Indian children by the New England Company near Brantford. His gift for languages led to an appointment as interpreter for the Anglican mission on the reserve. Eventually he held many important positions on the Six Nations Council and was a leader in the community until his death.

In 1853 Chief Johnson married a young English woman, Emily Howells, who had come to live with her sister at the Anglican mission on the reserve. As a wedding present, he built his bride a magnificent home which he called "Chiefswood." Chief Johnson and his English wife had four children, the youngest of whom was Emily Pauline. Although she was part white in her ancestry, since her great-grandmother was of Dutch descent and her mother English, Pauline considered herself wholly Indian: "I am a Red Indian and feel very proud of it. . . . I love everything Indian."[8] Pauline and her brothers and sisters were Indians by law as well as by choice. However, by Mohawk law Chief Johnson could not pass the chieftainship along to his sons because of their English mother,

212

*A portrait of the poet E. Pauline Johnson, showing her distinctive manner of dress in honour of her Mohawk heritage.*

for Emily Howells had not formally become a Mohawk by adoption as had Catherine Rolleston, two generations earlier.

Chief Johnson had developed the family's gift for languages which was so apparent in his father, and spoke and read not only English and the five other languages of the Six Nations but also French and German. Pauline Johnson was brought up in Chiefswood in a household where music and literature were appreciated, and in which there was a fine library well-stocked with good literature. There were many guests, among whom was the scientist Horatio Hale who described his visit as follows:

> The elegant and tasteful Indian home in the tree-embowered mansion overlooking the winding river, the cordial and dignified chief, the gentle English matron and the graceful and accomplished young Princesses – all making a picture so charming that visitors to Brantford, famous writers, actors and other public figures, eagerly sought an introduction there.[9]

Pauline, as a privileged princess of the Mohawks, was given the opportunity to develop her gift of writing. Her grandfather, John Smoke Johnson, instructed and entertained her with stories of her Mohawk heritage. He was a gifted storyteller as well as orator, and instilled in her an appreciation of Indian life and the history of her people. Among the stories he told were those of Joseph Brant, the Mohawk who led the "feathered Loyalists" from the Mohawk Valley of New York to their new settlement on the Grand River. Inspired by her grandfather's memories of Joseph Brant, Pauline wrote a poem in honour of the great Indian Loyalist leader. Written to commemorate the dedication of the memorial of the Brant monument in 1886, the poem reads:

On Dedication of a Memorial to Joseph Brant

Young Canada with mighty force sweeps on
To gain in power and strength before the dawn
That brings another era, when the sun
Shall rise again, but sadly shine upon
Her Indian graves and Indian memories.

*This picture taken by an unknown photographer in 1886 shows the ceremonial unveiling of the Brant Monument in Brantford, Ontario. For this occasion Pauline Johnson wrote her poem "On the Dedication of a Memorial to Joseph Brant," a tribute to Brant and the Loyalists of the Six Nations.*

For as the carmine in the twilight skies
Will fade as night comes on, as fades the race
That unto Might and doubtful Right gives place.
And as white clouds float hurriedly and high
Across the crimson of a sunset sky
Altho' their depths are foamy as the snow
Their beauty lies in their vermillion glow.
So, Canada, thy plumes were hardly won
Without allegiance from thy Indian son.
Thy glories, like the cloud, enhance their charm
With red reflections from the Mohawk's arm.
Then meet we as one common brotherhood
In peace and love, with purpose understood
To lift a lasting tribute to the name
Of Brant, who linked his own with Britain's fame.
Who bade his people leave their Valley Home
Where nature in her fairest aspects shone,
Where rolls the Mohawk River and the land
Is blest with every good from Heaven's hand,
To sweep the tide of home affections back
And love the land where waves the Union Jack.
What tho' that home no longer ours? Today
The Six Red Nations have their Canada.
And rest we here, no cause for us to rise
To seek protection under other skies.
Encircling us an arm both true and brave
Extends from far across the great salt wave.
Tho' but a woman's arm, 'tis firm, and strong
Enough to guard us from all fear of wrong,
An arm on which all British subjects lean –
The loving hand of England's noble Queen.

Chiefswood
October 8th, 1886                    Tekahionwake

# Chapter Thirteen

# David Franks
# (1720–1794)
# A Jewish Loyalist
# From Philadelphia

*A Colonial American merchant from a prominent New York mercantile family, David Franks founded a successful business in Philadelphia, and had extensive holdings in the unsettled Western lands of America. In the early years of the American Revolution he was deputy commissary of British prisoners for the rebels. Because of his dealings with England and with his brother, Moses, he was discharged from his duties, and finally ordered to leave Pennyslvania. Although a resident of Philadelphia, he had made frequent and lengthy visits to Montreal where he took a keen interest in the development of the Jewish community. Upon his expulsion from Pennsylvania he went to Montreal. After a short stay there, he left for England where he stayed until some time after the end of the Revolution, then returned to Philadelphia.*

David Franks was born into a family of wealthy merchants who had been prominent financiers for generations. His ancestral name was Franco or Franco-Dacosta in fifteenth-century Spain, but the surname was changed to Franks during the family's years in German-speaking areas of Europe after they were forced to leave Spain. This occurred late in the fifteenth century when King Ferdinand and Queen Isabella of Spain passed their Expulsion Edict by which all Jews were forced to be either converted to Catholicism or expelled from the country. These Sephardim, as Jews from Spain and Portugal were called, were distinguished by their wealth and highly developed cultural life in medieval times. When their expulsion drove them abroad, they took with them a cultural heritage which they continued to develop in the

*This eighteenth century portrait entitled "Children of Jacob and Abigail Franks" shows a young David Franks with his sister Phila.*

*A portrait of Jacob Franks, the American colonial merchant, father of the Loyalist David Franks of Philadelphia.*

lands where they settled. In their new surroundings they formed small Sephardic communities. David's father, Jacob Franks (1688-1769) was born in London. There, David's grandfather, Aaron Franks, was a broker for the Court, having been brought to England from Hanover to serve the German-speaking royal family. He had been a banker in Hanover, and acted as the King's personal financial adviser.

Jacob Franks arrived in New York from London in 1708 or 1709, with the intention of establishing an American branch of the family business. In 1711 he married Abigail Bilhah Levy, a member of one of the wealthiest and most prominent Jewish families of New York. Her family was also of Sephardic origin and had traded in furs as well as become bankers, and had also served in various public offices. The Levy and Franks families were prominent socially as well, and as members of the Sephardic community attended the same events as did the aristocracy.

Until 1720 it was only the Sephardic Jews who emigrated to New York. In the earliest days they came from the Netherlands to the Dutch colony in America, New Netherland. Later, when the English captured New Netherland, they came chiefly from England or from colonies in the West Indies or South America, in particular, Brazil. After 1720 the majority of the Jewish immigrants were not of Spanish or Portuguese origin but rather Ashkenazim, of East and Central European stock. While a few of these people came earlier than 1720, after that date almost all Jewish immigrants to colonial America were Ashkenazim who came from England; some of Polish or Hungarian origin but most of Germanic stock. They formed only a very small fraction of the number of immigrants who came to America, although they founded small but influential communities in New York, in Philadelphia, and in Newport, Rhode Island. They came to America chiefly for economic reasons.

About the year 1743, the Franks and Levy families settled in Philadelphia. Both families joined in the social activities of the Christian aristocracy of the city. David Franks' name is found on the list of those attending the first Assembly of 1748, the ball which was held annually

*This portrait of Phila Franks, David Franks' sister, is in the collection of the American Jewish Historical Society.*

and the greatest social event of Philadelphia. Abigail Levy Franks, David's mother, was greatly concerned with finding suitable mates for each of her seven children. In particular, she was distressed when in 1742 her eldest daughter, Phila, eloped with a New York neighbour, Oliver De Lancey, of French Huguenot descent, who was a Christian and who had Phila baptized. Then, only six months later, David married Margaret Evans of Philadelphia. Not long afterwards his mother died, "convinced that she had been a failure as a parent."[1] David and Margaret were the parents of two daughters, Abigail and Rebecca, described by the writer Stephen Birmingham, as follows:

> We see them in their portraits – Rebecca's by Thomas Sully, who later became Philadelphia's most popular society portraitist – pale, dark-haired with high cheekbones, long thin noses, and arresting eyes, white and swanlike necks, white bosoms swelling over low-cut dresses. They were unquestionably belles.[2]

Rebecca had many Tory friends who shared her interest in social life and held many lavish entertainments before the British evacuated Philadelphia in June 1778.

The people of Philadelphia had associated David Franks with his daughter's extravagance and party-loving, frivolous nature, which created a particularly poor impression in a colony at war. Nor did the activities of his brother-in-law, Oliver De Lancey, endear David to the rebels. In and around New York City, Oliver raised three battalions of Loyalists. De Lancey's Brigade was one of the largest Provincial Corps of the British Army, and Oliver was commissioned a brigadier-general. David had been selected as commissary to the British prisoners who were quartered in Philadelphia as prisoners of the rebels, and this fact, too, was held against him by many of his detractors.

These prisoners were "troops of the king of Great Britain" most of whom had been captured in Canada by the rebel forces in 1775. They were temporarily quartered in Connecticut, and later Pennsylvania, some in small towns and some in the city of Philadelphia. The rebels' Continental Congress appointed a committee to take charge of the prisoners, ordering:

That Mr. Franks of this city be permitted to supply
the troops now prisoners in this colony with provisions and other necessities at the expense of the crown,
and to sell his bills for such sums of money as are
necessary for that purpose. And that the committee
confer with Mr. Franks and know of him whether
he will undertake on the same terms to supply the
prisoners in the other colonies.[3]

Franks was given the name of "agent to the con-
tractors for victualling the troops of the king of Great
Britain." In February 1776 he contracted to victual the
troops who were then quartered in Reading, Pennsylvania. For two years he served in this capacity. However,
only six months after he began to provide the provisions
required, he had run into difficulties with payment for
his services. In October 1776 he asked for permission to
go to New York:

> . . . in order to lay his receipts and vouchers for the
> provisions furnished to the British prisoners, before
> the commissary-general, and obtain certificates to
> be presented to, and signed by the general of the
> British forces, without which he cannot be reim-
> bursed.[4]

His petition was granted, as long as he and his clerk,
who would accompany him, would:

> give their parole not to give any intelligence to the
> enemy, and that they return to this city.[5]

He does not appear to have made satisfactory arrangements, for his debts continued to increase as he
waited in vain for payment. Meanwhile, the British government was not paying because it felt that the responsibility for reimbursing Franks lay with the Continental
Congress, which was holding the prisoners. In theory at
least, prisoners-of-war were entitled to the same rations
as were issued to soldiers belonging to the country that
was holding them, and at that country's expense. Therefore, the British government felt that Franks' claim was
unjustified.

After he had paid for over 500,000 meals for British prisoners, without repayment, in spite of all his efforts to be reimbursed by the Lords of the Treasury, his affairs reached a point of crisis. When in September 1778 he was too short of cash to provide the prisoners' rations for the month, he was accused of treason by the rebels, and thrown into prison. Eventually he was released for want of evidence.

On 2 October 1780 he was held on a charge of secretly aiding the British. One of the few scraps of evidence which the rebels had found to prove his support for the British was a letter of his addressed to his brother, Moses Franks, in England and dated 19 September 1778. This letter had been intercepted by the rebels, and was mentioned in the *Journal of Congress* as follows:

> The committee to whom were referred the letters from David Franks, &c. brought in a report: whereupon the letter from David Franks, Esq. commissary of British prisoners, to Moses Franks, Esq. of London, enclosed under cover to Capt. Thomas Moore of General Delancey's regiment, being read, . . . [6]

The committee ruled that Franks' letter, while over two years old, was evidence that he was hostile to the security of the United States, in effect an enemy of American liberty, in having attempted to transmit a letter secretly to New York City, with its British garrison. Franks had betrayed the Continental Congress, and was no longer a fit person to serve as a commissary to the British prisoners. The committee wrote an order for "Major Genl Arnold" to have Franks arrested and conveyed to Philadelphia to be held in jail until the Congress should decide what to do with him. Apparently the committee was unaware that Benedict Arnold, who had commanded the rebel post at West Point, on the Hudson River, had defected to the British at New York City on 25 September 1780, a week earlier. The order to Arnold also indicates that Franks was not in Philadelphia at that time. However, he was apprehended and brought there.

This time he was ordered to leave the country. Not only was he exiled, but to be certain that he would not return before the end of the war, his entire fortune was seized. This was a severe loss, for as a successful businessman he had accumulated the sizeable fortune of 200,000 pounds, in spite of the large amount he thought the British owed him.

In October 1780 he was sent to New York, his daughter Rebecca with him. There, Rebecca continued to pursue an active social life, now in New York Tory society. She sent frequent, amusing letters to her family members. In these she was highly critical of New York society, comparing it unfavourably with her own circle in Philadelphia. Meanwhile, her father desperately tried to regain the money owed to him, an effort in which he was never successful. He was now a ruined man, and in later years lived on small loans from fellow Sephardim.

From New York he travelled to Montreal, where he settled for some time among friends and relatives in the small Jewish community there. In Montreal was a relative, the merchant Abraham Franks, who had left Philadelphia before the revolution to found a business there. As in Philadelphia, some of the Jews were Loyalists, while others supported the American cause. One member of the family, David Salisbury Franks, who favoured the rebels, had returned to Pennsylvania years before, because he had helped the rebels in 1775-1776 during their unsuccessful invasion of Quebec.

After spending a short time in Montreal, David Franks sailed for England where he spent the remainder of the war. He made many unsuccessful attempts to be compensated for his great losses.

However, Rebecca Franks made a brilliant marriage, becoming the bride of one of her titled suitors, Sir Henry Johnson. She was welcomed into London society, as she had been in Philadelphia and New York. Her descendants were the Johnsons of Bath, who served by tradition as officers in the British Army. Of her nine grandsons, with the exception of one who became an Episcopal clergyman, all became army officers, numbering three generals, one major general, one lieutenant general, two colonels, and one captain.

Her beautiful sister Abigail made an equally brilliant marriage to Andrew Hamilton, a Philadelphia law-

*The home of David Franks in Woodford, Pennsylvania.*

yer of renown. Among her descendants were members of many distinguished families, both American and English. By the end of the eighteenth century, all the members of David Franks' family had intermarried into Christian families and had lost their place in the distinctive Sephardic communities of the colonies and of the mother country, England.

David Franks, their father, is said to have renounced the Jewish faith when he married Margaret Evans. However, he remained in close contact with the Sephardic communities of the cities in which he lived, and contributed to the fund which was raised for the construction of the first synagogue in Montreal. Only a year or two before his death he stated that he was a Jew, taking his oath upon the five books of Moses. In 1793 or 1794 he died, probably in England in 1794 rather than of yellow fever in Philadelphia in 1793 as previously believed, although the exact circumstances of his death have not been determined with any certainty.

As has been pointed out by the Canadian author B.G. Sack, "His profound sympathy with the English cause which he in no wise attempted to conceal, ultimately cost him his high social position and his wealth."[7] David Franks deserves to be numbered among Loyal Americans who suffered greatly during the American Revolution, and his story is an example of the tribulations that could befall a civilian Loyalist in those difficult times.

# Notes

## Chapter One

1. *Atlas of Early American History – The Revolutionary Era, 1760-1790* (Princeton, N.J.: Princeton University Press, 1976), pp. 24-25.
2. Letter quoted by Milton M. Klein in "Shaping the American Tradition: The Microcosm of New York," in *New York History*, LVIX, No. 2 (April 1978), p. 188.
3. Andrew Burnaby, *Travels Through North America* (New York: A. Wessels, 1904), p. 117.
4. Dutch West Indian Company to Peter Stuyvesant, April 16, 1663, in E. C. Corwin, ed., *Ecclesiastical Records of the State of New York*, I, p. 530.
5. Algemeen Rijksarchief, Den Haag, Resolutiën van de Staten van Holland en West Friesland, 55, folio 72, quoted in Oliver A. Rink, "The People of New Netherland: Notes on Non-English Immigration to New York in the Seventeenth Century," in *New York History*, LXII, no. 1 (January 1981), p. 9.
6. *Ibid.*, pp. 52-53.
7. "The Ethnographical Elements of Ontario," in *Ontario Historical Society. Papers and Records*, III, 1901, p. 180.
8. Harmut Froeschle, "German Immigration into Canada. A Survey," in *German-Canadian Yearbook*, 1981, p. 16.

## Chapter Two

1. Kenneth Coleman, *The American Revolution in Georgia 1763-1789*, (Athens Ga.: University of Georgia Press, 1958), pp. 100, 108-9. The author describes the activities of the Florida Rangers of the Southern Department.
2. Mary Beacock Fryer, *King's Men: the Soldier Founders of Ontario*, (Toronto: Dundurn Press, 1980), pp. 14-17, 26-28.
3. Haldimand Papers, British Museum, London, Add. Mss. 21819, p. 125, Haldimand to Sir John Johnson, 10 August 1780.

## Chapter Three

1. The name "Northern Netherlands" refers to the seven northern provinces – Holland, Zeeland, Utrecht, Groningen, Overijssel, Gelderland, and Friesland – which concluded the Union of Utrecht in 1579. Two years later they declared themselves independent of Spain. The Southern Netherlands, which was approximately the same area as modern Belgium, remained under Spanish domination for many more years. Spain and Austria alternately ruled the Southern Netherlands until 1795, when all of the Netherlands came under the power of the French Republic. All the provinces of Holland and Belgium were united in 1814 to form the United Kingdom of the Netherlands. This arrangement lasted until 1830, when the southern provinces broke away and formed the Kingdom of Belgium.
2. Gerald De Jong, *The Dutch in America, 1609-1974* (Boston: Twayne, 1975), p. 46.
3. This is the name given in certain Reformed churches to the governing body of a certain area, made up of church officials and selected elders representing various districts; it can also refer to the area governed by the classis.

4. It is now in the collection of the King's Museum of Liverpool, England, where it is one of a number of displays related to the military career of Colonel Arent Schuyler De Peyster, whose regimental headquarters were in Liverpool.

5. The former commandant, Lieutenant Governor Henry Hamilton, had taken a small force to fight rebel colonials in the border country between what are now Indiana and Illinois. There he had been taken a prisoner, and his fate was unknown. When De Peyster arrived in Detroit in 1779 the American Revolution was well under way, and there was fear of an attack on the fort, which had been in British control since the capitulation of the French in 1760.

6. The original John Askin Papers are held in the Burton Historical Collection of the Detroit Public Library. A selected number were edited by M. M. Quaife, and published in two volumes in Detroit in 1928 and 1931.

7. *Michigan Pioneer Collection*, X, 1888, p. 540.8. David Zeisberger, *Diary of David Zeisberger*, trans. and ed. Eugene F. Bliss (Cincinnati: Robert Clarke, 1885), I, p. 33.

8. David Zeisberger, *Diary of David Zeisberger*, I, p. 32.

9. Elma E. Gray, *Wilderness Christians* (Toronto: Macmillan, 1956), pp. 70-71.

10. *Ibid.*

11. Hog Island was later renamed Belle Isle, the name by which this American island in the Detroit River is known today.

12. The name "Moneso" is probably a misinterpretation of De Peyster's handwriting, with the word being correctly read as "Monsieur".

13. John Askin, *The John Askin Papers*, ed. M. M. Quaife (Detroit: Detroit Library Commission, 1931), II, p. 407.

14. William Will, *Robert Burns as a Volunteer* (Aberdeen: Bon-Accord, 1927).

15. Arent Schuyler De Peyster, *Miscellanies by an Officer* (Dumfries: C. Munro, 1813), pp. 35-36. The explanatory notes appended to the poem were written by De Peyster for the 1813 edition of this book. The Red River is now known as River Rouge.

16. Letter 693, in *The Letters of Robert Burns* (Oxford: Clarendon Press, 1931), II, p. 319.

17. Robert Burns, *The Poems and Songs of Robert Burns*, ed. James Kinsley (Oxford: Clarendon Press, 1968), II, pp. 809-810.

18. Dumfries *Courier*, Dec. 1822.

**Chapter Four**

1. Frederick C. Hamil, *Valley of the Lower Thames, 1640-1850* (Toronto: University of Toronto Press, 1951), p. 349.

2. Marion Field Belanger, "The Field Family – Early Ontario Settlers" in *Families*, XXII, 2, 1983, pp. 114-115.

3. James Smith, *An Account of the Remarkable Occurrences in the Life and Travels of Col. James Smith* (Cincinnati: Robert Clarke, 1870), pp. 79-80.

4. *Commemorative Biographical Record of the County of Kent, Ontario* (Toronto: J. H. Beers, 1904), p. 4.

5. Journal of Benjamin Mortimer, August 1798 as quoted in Elma E. Gray, *Wilderness Christians* (Toronto: Macmillan, 1956), p. 79.

6. Eugene F. Bliss, ed. and trans., *Diary of David Zeisberger* (Cincinnati: Robert Clarke, 1885), II, p. 229.

7. *Ibid.*, p. 254.

8. *Ibid.*, pp. 219-220.

9. Moravian Church Diary 17 July 1812 as quoted in Elma E. Gray, *Wilderness Christians*, p. 213.

## Chapter Five

1. Francis Moore, *Travels into the Inland Part of Africa* (London: E. Cave, 1738) as quoted in Henry F. Reeve, *The Gambia* (London: Smith, Elder, 1912), pp. 73-74.
2. *Ibid.*, p. 75.
3. Information supplied by Mrs. Sheila Wilson, who specializes in St. Catharines local history and especially the life of "Black Dick" (Pierpoint).
4. Captain Fowler, D.A.Q.M.G., to Colonel Baynes, 29 May 1813 as quoted in Ernest Green, "Upper Canada's Black Defenders," in Ontario Historical Society *Papers and Records*, vol. XXVII, p. 368.
5. It is possible that Richard Pierpoint had heard of the fact that in 1791 almost 1,000 Loyalist blacks accepted the British government's offer to send them to Sierra Leone in Africa, where it was planned to found a settlement for free blacks. Another group of 550 blacks, known as the Maroons, were sent from Nova Scotia to Sierra Leone in 1800. The blacks in both of these groups found it difficult to adjust to the climate of Nova Scotia.
6. Public Archives of Canada. Upper Canada sundries, 1821.
7. Ontario Archives, RG 22, Niagara North Estate File, Richard Pawpine, Grantham, 27 September 1838.

## Chapter Six

1. Benjamin Franklin, *Papers of Benjamin Franklin* (New Haven, Conn.: Yale University Press), IV, p. 65.
2. *Ibid.*
3. *Ibid.*, p. 118.
4. John Adams, *Diary and Autobiography of John Adams* (Cambridge, Mass.: Harvard University Press, 1961), I, pp. 128, 280, 290, 292, 302-304; II, p. 52.
5. William S. Pattee, *A History of Old Braintree and Quincy* (Quincy, Mass.: Green & Prescott, 1878), p. 389.
6. *Province in Rebellion*, ed. by L. K. Wroth (Cambridge, Mass.: Harvard University Press, 1975), pp. 2078-2080.
7. "Refugees of 1776" in *Massachusetts Historical Society. Proceedings, 1880-1881*, XVIII, p. 268.
8. Ontario, Bureau of Archives. *Second Report: Annual Report for the Year 1904*, I (Toronto: King's Printer, 1905), pp. 900-901.
9. Harry Piers and Donald MacKay, *Master Goldsmiths and Silversmiths of Nova Scotia* (Halifax: Antiquarian Club, 1948), p. 123.

## Chapter Seven

1. There are two quite different genealogies which trace the ancestry of the Rapalje family in one case to Gaspard Coley de Rapalje, born in France in 1505 and in the other to Georges Rapareillet, born in Valenciennes in the independent countship of Hainaut (now in the department of Nord in France) in 1604. Both of these men were Protestants who sought refuge in the Netherlands. The author of this book has chosen to accept evidence that Joris Janszen Rapalje was a descendant of Gaspard Coley de Rapalje of Chatillon sur Loire in France. This seems a more acceptable lineage since church records of the Rapareillet family do not show that Georges Rapareillet had two brothers Antonie and Willem (Antoine and Guillaume)

while these brothers played a prominent role in Joris de Rapalje's life in New Netherland. The names of these three brothers, Joris, Antonie, and Willem, are recorded in the Dutch colonial records and there seems to be no doubt of the relationship between them.

2. Ernest Cruickshank, "The Loyalists of New York," in *United Empire Loyalists' Association of Ontario. Annual Transactions*, I, 1898, p. 58.

3. Agnes E. R. Taylor, "A Norfolk County U.E. Loyalist – Captain Abraham A. Rapelje," in *United Empire Loyalists' Association of Ontario. Annual Transactions*, V, 1903/04, p. 67.

4. Archives of Ontario. Memorandum Book of Abraham A. Rapelje, Capt. 1st Flank Co., 2nd Regiment, Norfolk Militia, War of 1812-14. MU 2099.

5. Agnes E. R. Taylor, "A Norfolk County U. E. Loyalist," pp. 73-74.

## Chapter Eight

1. From Captain Felix O'Neill's journal, quoted in Charles Petrie, *The Jacobite Movement: The Last Phase, 1716-1807* (London: Eyre & Spottiswood, 1950), pp. 129-130.

2. *Ibid.*, pp. 130-131.

3. *Ibid.*, p. 131.

4. *Ibid.*, p. 132.

5. The Baron Porcelli. *The White Cockade*, (London: Hutchinson, 1950), pp. 236-238.

6. Father MacAdam, quoted in Charles W. Dunn, *Highland Settler: A Portrait of the Scottish Gael in Nova Scotia*, (Toronto: University of Toronto Press, 1953), p. 14.

7. Thomas Pennant. *A Tour in Scotland, and Voyage to the Hebrides.* 2 v. (Chester, England: J. Monk, 1774-1776), quoted in Donald MacKay, *Scotland Farewell: The People of the Hector*, (Toronto: McGraw-Hill Ryerson, 1980, pp. 59-60.

8. Letters from Flora Macdonald to Mrs. Mackenzie of Devlin, 24 July 1780 and 3 July 1782, quoted in Compton Mackenzie, *Prince Charlie and His Ladies*, (New York: Knopf, 1935), pp. 161-163.

## Chapter Nine

1. Manuscript written by Mrs. Eliza Smith Orpin in 1876, quoted in: Kennedy B. Wainwright, "A Comparative Study in Nova Scotian Rural Economy 1788-1872, Based on Recently Discovered Books of Account of Old Firms in King's County, Nova Scotia," in *Nova Scotia Historical Society. Collections*, XXX, 1954, pp. 78-119.

2. *Ibid.*, pp. 82-83.

3. Ontario. Bureau of Archives. *Second Report: Annual Report for the Year 1904*, I (Toronto: King's Printer, 1905), pp. 537-538.

4. Wainwright, p. 84.

5. *Ibid.*, p. 106.

## Chapter Ten

1. Oscar Kuhns, *The German and Swiss Settlements of Colonial Pennsylvania*, (New York: Henry Holt and Co., 1901), p. 6.

2. John Ferrar, *History of the City of Limerick*, 2nd ed. 1767, quoted in Eula C. Lapp, *To Their Heirs Forever*, (Belleville: Mika, 1977), p. 48.

3. John Wesley, *The Works of the Reverend John Wesley, A. M.*, (London: John Mason, 1849) II, p. 429.

4. Letter by C. Manson entitled "The Emburys and Hecks in Canada" published in *Christian Advocate*, November, 1866, quoted by Eula C. Lapp in *To Their Heirs Forever*, p. 113.

5. W.H. Withrow, *Makers of Methodism*, (Toronto: Wm. Briggs, 1898), X.
6. Eula C. Lapp, *To Their Heirs Forever*, p. 174.
7. Public Record Office, London. AO 13-14. Memorial of John Wilson.
8. Public Archives of Canada, Ottawa. War Office 28, vol. 4, p. 266.
9. Lt. Genl. John Burgoyne, *A State of the Expedition From Canada*, (London: J. Almon 1780), Appendix, Burgoyne's Plan of Battle.
10. New York State Library, Albany, MSS 3591, "Return of the third company, Queen's Loyal Rangers, after the Battle of Bennington."
11. Public Archives of Canada, Ottawa, War Office 28, vol. 9, p. 95, "Memorial of Justus Sherwood, March 9, 1778."
12. Eula C. Lapp, *To Their Heirs Forever*, p. 174.
13. *Ibid.*, p. 240.
14. *Centennial of Canadian Methodism*, (Toronto: William Briggs, 1891), pp. 56-57.
15. Eula C. Lapp, *To Their Heirs Forever*, p. 305.

**Chapter Eleven**
1. Lorne A. Pierce, "The German Loyalist in Upper Canada." In *The Canadian Magazine*, LV no. 4, August 1929, pp. 290-296.
2. J. J. Talman, ed., *Loyalist Narratives From Upper Canada*, (Toronto: The Champlain Society, 1946), "Reminiscences of Captain James Dittrick" p. 63.
3. Mary Beacock Fryer, *King's Men: the Soldier Founders of Ontario*, (Toronto: Dundurn Press, 1980), p. 135.
4. Public Archives of Canada, Ottawa, Colonial Office M.G. 11, "Q" Series, vol. 13, p. 331.
5. Fryer, *King's Men*, pp. 79-81.
6. *Ibid.*, pp. 137-138.
7. *Ibid.* pp. 159-69.
8. Ontario Bureau of Archives, *Second Report: Annual Report for the Year 1904*, II, (Toronto: King's Printer, 1905), Claim of William Pickard, pp. 963-964.
9. Dittrick Family Bible.
10. J. J. Talman, *Loyalist Narratives*, pp. 62-69.
11. *Illustrated Historical Atlas of the Counties of Lincoln and Welland, Ontario*, (Toronto: H.R. Page, 1876), p. 13.
12. Ontario Archives, Toronto, Upper Canada Land Petitions.

**Chapter Twelve**
1. Colonel Schuyler was a distinguished member of the Dutch community of the Hudson River Valley who, for many years, acted as the British official in charge of Indian affairs. He was genuinely interested in the welfare of the Indians and appreciated their friendship and support. There is no doubt that Colonel Arent De Peyster was inspired by the earlier work of Colonel Schuyler, to whom he was closely related through his mother's side of the family, when he, too, became on excellent terms with the Western Indians and succeeded in keeping them as loyal friends of the British throughout the years of revolution.
2. Evelyn H. C. Johnson, "Chief John Smoke Johnson," in *Ontario Historical Society. Papers and Records*, XII, 1914, p. 103.
3. *Ibid.*, p. 104.
4. *Ibid.*, p. 105.
5. W. Jamieson, "The Saga of the Queen Anne Silver Plate," in *The Loyalist Gazette*, Autumn 1970, p. 7.

6. Patrick Campbell, *Travels in the Interior Inhabited Parts of North America in the Years 1791 and 1792* (Toronto: The Champlain Society, 1937), pp. 167-169.
7. F. Douglas Reville, *History of the County of Brant* (Brantford: Hurley Printing Company, 1920), p. 56.
8. Words spoken by Pauline Johnson to a London reporter on her first visit to England in 1894, quoted in, Marcus Van Steen, *Pauline Johnson: Her Life and Work* (Toronto: Hodder and Stoughton, 1965), p. 3.
9. *Ibid.*, p. 6.

## Chapter Thirteen
1. Stephen Birmingham, *The Grandees: America's Sephardic Elite* (New York: Harper & Row, 1971), p. 166.
2. *Ibid.*, pp. 166-167.
3. Journal of Congress, 2 December 1775, quoted in The American Jewish Historical Society, *The Jewish Experience in America* (New York: KTAV Publishing House, 1969), I, p. 324.
4. *Ibid.*, 24 October 1776, p. 325.
5. *Ibid.*
6. *Ibid.*, 19 September 1778, p. 325.
7. B. G. Sack, *History of the Jews in Canada* (Montreal: Harvest House, 1965), p. 62.

# Selected Bibliography

**Chapter One**

Allen, Robert S. *The Loyal Americans*. Ottawa: National Museums, 1983.

Allen, Robert. *Loyalist Literature: An Annotated Bibliographic Guide to the Writings on the Loyalists of the American Revolution*. Toronto: Dundurn, 1982.

American Council of Learned Societies. *Surnames in the United States, Census of 1790: An Analysis of National Origins of the Population*. Baltimore: Genealogical Publishing Company, 1969.

Blakely, Phyllis R., ed. and John N. Grant, ed. *Eleven Exiles: Accounts of Loyalists of the American Revolution*. Toronto: Dundurn, 1982.

Cappon, Lester J., ed. *Atlas of Early American History: The Revolutionary Era, 1760-1790*. Princeton, New Jersey: Princeton University Press, 1976.

Fryer, Mary Beacock. *King's Men: The Soldier Founders of Ontario*. Toronto: Dundurn, 1980.

Fryer, Mary Beacock, and William A. Smy. *Rolls of the Provincial (Loyalist) Corps, Canadian Command, American Revolutionary Period*. Toronto: Dundurn, 1981.

Fryer, Mary Beacock, ed. and Charles J. Humber, ed. *Loyal She Remains: A Pictorial History of Ontario*. Toronto: The United Empire Loyalists' Association of Canada, 1984.

Mika, Nick and Helma Mika. *United Empire Loyalists, Pioneers of Upper Canada*. 2nd ed. Belleville, Ontario: Mika, 1976.

Nova Scotia. Public Archives. *The Loyalists Guide: The Annotated Guide & Loyalists Sources in the Public Archives of Nova Scotia*. Halifax: Public Archives of Nova Scotia, 1983.

Power, Michael. *A History of the Roman Catholic in the Niagara Peninsula, 1615-1815*. Windsor: Roman Catholic Diocese of St. Catharines, 1983.

Sowell, Thomas. *Ethnic America: A History*. New York: Basic Books, 1981.

Wilson, Bruce: *As She Began: An Illustrated Introduction to Loyalist Ontario*. Toronto: Dundurn, 1981.

**Chapter Two**

Coleman, Kenneth. *The American Revolution in Georgia 1763-1789*. Athens, Ga.: University of Georgia Press, 1958.

Fryer, Mary Beacock. *King's Men: the Soldier Founders of Ontario*. Toronto: Dundurn Press, 1980.

**Chapter Three**

Armour, David. "A White Beaver for the Colonel." In *Michigan Natural Resources*, July-Aug. 1973, pp. 11-13.

Askin, John. *The John Askin Papers*, edited by M. M. Quaife. Detroit: Detroit Public Library, 1928-1931.

Belknap, Waldron P. *The De Peyster Genealogy*. Boston: privately printed, 1956.

Burns, Robert. *The Poems and Songs of Robert Burns*, edited by James Kinsley. Oxford: Clarendon Press, 1968, 3v.

De Jong, Gerald. *The Dutch in America, 1609-1974*. Boston: Twayne, 1975.

De Peyster, A. S. *Miscellanies by an Officer*. Dumfries: C. Munro, 1813.

De Peyster, Henry. "The Pre-American Ancestry of the De Peyster Family." In *The New York Genealogical and Biographical Record*, LXX, no. 3, July 1939; LXX, no. 4,October 1939, pp. 313-331.

Fuller, Robert M. "Major De Peyster, British Commandant of Detroit." In *Western Ontario Historical Notes*, v.10, n.3, September 1952, pp. 102-107.

Gray, Elma E. *Wilderness Christians: The Moravian Missions to the Delaware Indians*. Toronto: Macmillan, 1956.

Will, William. *Robert Burns as a Volunteer*. Aberdeen: Bon-Accord, 1927.

Zeisberger, David. *Diary of David Zeisberger, a Moravian Missionary Among the Indians of Ohio*, translated from the original German manuscript by Eugene F. Bliss. Cincinnati: R. Clarke, 1885.

## Chapter Four

Belanger, Marion F. "The Field Family – Early Ontario Settlers." In *Families*, XXII, 2, 1983, pp. 114-118.

Gray, Elma E. *Wilderness Christians: The Moravian Mission to the Delaware Indians*. Toronto: Macmillan, 1956.

Hamil, Fred Coyne. *The Valley of the Lower Thames, 1640 to 1850*. Toronto: University of Toronto Press, 1951.

Ladell, John and Monica. *Ontario's Century Farms, Past & Present*. Toronto: Macmillan, 1979.

Magee, Joan. *A Dutch Heritage: 200 Years of Dutch Presence in the Windsor-Detroit Border Region*. Toronto: Dundurn, 1983.

## Chapter Five

Ajayi, J. F. A. and Crowder, Michael. *History of West Africa*, I. New York: Columbia University Press, 1972.

Green, Ernest. "Upper Canada's Black Defenders." In Ontario Historical Society *Papers and Records*, XXVII, 1931, pp. 365-391.

Hill, Daniel G. *The Freedom-Seekers: Blacks in Early Canada*. Agincourt: Book Society of Canada, 1981.

Jackson, John N. *St. Catharines, Its Early Years*. Belleville: Mika, 1976.

Johnston, Harry. *Pioneers in West Africa*. London: Blackie, 1912.

Rancon, A. *Le Bondou, étude de géographie et d'histoire soudaniennes de 1681 à nos jours*. Bordeaux: Gounouilhou, 1894.

Reeve, Henry Fenwick. *The Gambia: Its History, Ancient, Mediaeval, and Modern*. London: Smith, Elder, 1912.

Stanley, George F. C. *The War of 1812: Land Operations*. Toronto: Macmillan, 1983.

Winks, Robin W. *The Blacks in Canada: A History*. Montreal: McGill-Queen's University Press, 1971.

## Chapter Six

Etter, Thomas C. The Etter Family. Unpublished manuscript. American Etter Society Archives.

*Etter Family Register of Ferenbalm, Kerzers, Murten, Switzerland: (The Reichen Report)*. Houston, Texas: American Etter Society, 1965.

Pattee, William S. *A History of Old Braintree and Quincy*. Quincy, Mass.: Green & Prescott, 1878.

Public Archives of Nova Scotia. Transcript of letter from Peter Etter to Sir Frederick Haldimand, written from Denmark Street, Halifax, dated 15 August 1778. British Military Correspondence: Haldimand Papers. RG 1, CCCLXVI.

*Schweizerisches Familienbuch*. Zurich: Genealogisches Institut Zwicky, 1947.

Stayner, C. S. Genealogy of the Etter Family of Chester. Unpublished manuscript. Public Archives of Nova Scotia.

## Chapter Seven
Cruikshank, Ernest. "The Loyalists of New York." In *United Empire Loyalists' Association of Ontario. Annual Transactions*, I, 1898, pp. 49-62.

Holgate, Jerome B. *American Genealogy: A History of Some of the Early Settlers of North America and Their Descendants*. Albany: Joel Munsell, 1848.

Owen, E. A. *Pioneer Sketches of Long Point Settlement, or, Norfolk's Foundation Builders and Their Family Genealogies*. Toronto: William Briggs, 1898.

Reaman, G. Elmore. *The Trail of the Huguenots in Europe, the United States, South Africa, and Canada*. Baltimore: Genealogical Publishing Company, 1966.

Taylor, Agnes E. R. "A Norfolk County U. E. Loyalist – Captain Abraham A. Rapelje." In *United Empire Loyalists' Association of Ontario. Annual Transactions*, V, 1904/04, pp. 66-74.

## Chapter Eight
Dunn, Charles W. *Highland Settler: A Portrait of the Scottish Gael in Nova Scotia*. Toronto: University of Toronto Press, 1953.

MacDonald, Allan R. *The Truth About Flora MacDonald*, ed. by D. MacKinnon. Inverness: Northern Chronicle, 1939.

Mackenzie, Compton. *Prince Charlie and His Ladies*. New York: Knopf, 1935.

Petrie, Charles. *The Jacobite Movement: The Last Phase, 1716-1807*. London: Eyre & Spottiswood, 1950.

Porcelli, The Baron. *The White Cockade*. London: Hutchinson and Co., 1950.

Vining, Elizabeth. *Flora: A Biography*. Philadelphia: Lippincott, 1966.

## Chapter Nine
De Breffny, Brian De, ed. *The Irish World: The History and Cultural Achievements of the Irish People*. London: Thames and Hudson, 1977.

Eaton, Arthur Wentworth Hamilton. *The History of King's County, Nova Scotia*. Reprint edition. Belleville, Ont.: Mika, 1972.

McNutt, W. S. *The Atlantic Provinces: The Emergence of Colonial Society, 1712-1857*. Toronto: McClelland Stewart, 1965.

Ontario. Bureau of Archives. *Second Report: Annual Report for the Year 1904*, I (Toronto: King's Printer, 1905), pp. 537-538.

Public Archives of Nova Scotia. Business Papers: Kentville. Henry Magee, Merchant, 1788-1806 MG 3, 237-238.

Wainwright, Kennedy B. "A Comparative Study in Nova Scotian Rural Economy 1788-1872, Based on Recently Discovered Books of Account of Old Firms in King's County, Nova Scotia." In *Nova Scotia Historical Society. Collections*, XXX, 1954, pp. 78-119.

## Chapter Ten
Fryer, Mary Beacock. *Buckskin Pimpernel*, a biography of Justus Sherwood. Toronto: Dundurn Press, 1981.

Fryer, Mary Beacock. *King's Men: the Soldier Founders of Ontario*. Toronto: Dundurn Press, 1980.

Kuhns, Oscar. *The German and Swiss Settlement of Colonial Pennsylvania: A Study of the So-Called Pennsylvania Dutch*. New York: Henry Holt and Company, 1901.

Lapp, Eula C. *To Their Heirs Forever*. 3rd. ed. Belleville, Ontario: Mika, 1979.

Methodist Church in Canada. *Centennial of Canadian Methodism*. Toronto: William Briggs, 1891.

Playter, George F. *The History of Methodism in Canada*. Toronto: Anson Green, 1862.

Sanderson, J. E. *The First Century of Methodism in Canada*. 2 vols. Toronto: William Briggs, 1908.

Sutherland, Alexander. *Methodism in Canada: Its Work and Story*. Toronto: Methodist Mission Rooms, 1904.

Tucker, W. Bowman. *The Romance of the Palatine Millers: A Tale of Palatine Irish-Americans and United Empire Loyalists*. Montreal: W. B. Tucker, 1929.

## Chapter Eleven

Dittrick Family Bible.

Fryer, Mary Beacock. *King's Men: the Soldier Founders of Ontario*. Toronto: Dundurn Press, 1980.

*Illustrated Historical Atlas of the Counties of Lincoln and Welland, Ontario*. Toronto: H.R. Page, 1876.

Ontario Bureau of Archives. *Second Report: Annual Report for the Year 1904*. Toronto, 1905.

Pierce, Lorne A. "The German Loyalist in Upper Canada." In *The Canadian Magazine*, LV no. 4, August 1929.

*St. Catharines Centennial History*. St. Catharines: Advance Printing, 1967.

Smy, William A., and Mary Beacock Fryer. *Rolls of the Provincial Corps, Canadian Command, American Revolutionary Period*. Toronto: Dundurn Press, 1981.

Talman, J. J. ed. *Loyalist Narratives From Upper Canada*. Toronto: The Champlain Society, 1946.

Turner, Wesley B. and Morris Zaslow, eds. *The Defended Border: Upper Canada and the War of 1812*. Toronto: Macmillan, 1964.

## Chapter Twelve

Faux, David. "Documenting Six Nations Indian Ancestry." In *Families*, XX, No. 1, 1981, pp. 31-42.

Graymont, Barbara. "Thayendanegea." In *Dictionary of Canadian Biography*. Toronto: University of Toronto Press, 1983, V, pp. 803-811.

Johnson, Evelyn H. C. "Chief John Smoke Johnson." In *Ontario Historical Society. Papers and Records*, XII, 1914, pp. 102-113.

Johnston, Charles M., ed. *The Valley of the Six Nations: A Collection of Documents on the Indian Lands of the Grand River*. Toronto: The Champlain Society, 1964.

Leighton, Douglas. "George Henry Martin Johnson." In *Dictionary of Canadian Biography*. Toronto: University of Toronto Press, 1982, XI, pp. 451-453.

Leighton, Douglas. "John Johnson." In *Dictionary of Canadian Biography*. Toronto: University of Toronto Press, 1982, XI, pp. 453-454.

Lydekker, John Wolfe. *The Faithful Mohawks*. Port Washington, N.Y.: Ira J. Friedman, 1968.

Reville, F. Douglas. *History of the County of Brant*. Brantford: Hurley Printing Co., 1920.

Van Steen, Marcus. "Brantford's Royal Chapel." In *Canadian Geographical Journal*, LVII, no. 4, October 1958, pp. 136-141.

Van Steen, Marcus. *Pauline Johnson: Her Life and Work*. Toronto: Hodder and Stoughton, 1965.

## Chapter Thirteen

American Jewish Historical Society. *The Jewish Experience in America*. Vol. I. New York: KTAV Publishing House, 1969.

Birmingham, Stephen. *The Grandees: America's Sephardic Elite*. New York: Harper & Row, 1971.

Marcus, Jacob R. *The Colonial American Jew, 1492-1776*. Detroit: Wayne State University Press, 1970.

Rezneck, Samuel. *Unrecognized Patriots: The Jews in the American Revolution*. Westport, Conn.: Greenwood Press, 1975.

Sack, B. G. *History of the Jews in Canada*. Montreal: Harvest House, 1965.

# Illustration, Photograph
# and Map Credits

Cover: Theo Lubbers, United Empire Loyalist Memorial Window, Grace United Church, Napanee, Ontario. Stained glass window, 1983. G. Webster.

Backcover: H. Charles Devasagayam, "Ethnic Origins and Religious Groups, c. 1784". Manuscript map, 1984. J. Magee.

page 17.   (Frontispiece) William Berczy, "Portrait of Joseph Brant". Oil on canvas, 1797. Negative no. 5777. National Gallery of Canada.

page 18.   Artist unknown, "Plan Topographique Du Detroit et des eaux qui forment la Jonction du Lac Erie avec le Lac Saint Clair . . . 1796." Photograph of watercolour. NMC 3097, National Map Collection, Public Archives of Canada. Original with Service historique de l'Armée, Paris, 7B61.

page 24.   H. Charles Devasagayam, "Loyalist Settlement in Nova Scotia, Lower Canada, and Upper Canada". Manuscript map, 1984. J. Magee.

page 27.   Artist unknown, "Portrait of Jacques (James) Bâby". Photograph of oil on canvas. Original not extant. Hiram Walker Historical Museum, Windsor, Ontario.

page 28.   Anonymous, "Hon. James Bâby's Residence, Sandwich, August 1887". Hiram Walker Historical Museum, Windsor, Ontario.

page 32.   Butler's Rangers Button, found at Matthew Elliott Site, 1969. Leonard Kroon, University of Windsor.

page 34.   Theo Lubbers, United Empire Loyalist Memorial Window, Grace United Church, Napanee, Ontario. Stained glass window (detail), 1983. G. Webster.

page 35.   Artist unknown, "Portrait of Bishop Alexander Macdonnell". Oil on canvas. Archival Centre, Roman Catholic Diocese of Kingston.

page 38.   Artist unknown, "Portrait of Arent Schuyler De Peyster". Oil on canvas, ca. 1780. Burton Historical Collection, Detroit Public Library.

page 39.   Jan van de Velde, "Grote Markt met het stadhuis". Etching from original painting by P. Saenredam, ca. 1627-1628. Rijksarchief in Noord-Holland, Haarlem, The Netherlands.

page 41.   Artist unknown, "De Peyster House, Pearl St., New York". In Arent Schuyler De Peyster, *Miscellanies by an Officer* (Dumfries: C. Munro, 1813), p. CLXVII.

page 43.   Beaver skin. King's Gallery, Liverpool, England.

page 43.   Tomahawk. King's Gallery, Liverpool, England.

page 52.   Artist unknown, "Mavis Grove (near Dumfries) Residence of Col. Arent Schuyler De Peyster, B.A.". In Arent Schuyler De Peyster, *Miscellanies by an Officer* (Dumfries: C. Munro, 1813), p. CCII.

page 54.   P. J. Lloyd, "Loyalist Settlement in Ontario". In Bruce Wilson, *As She Began* (Toronto: Dundurn, 1981), p. 69.

page 56.   Farm house, Dalfsen, The Netherlands. Dalfsen Photographers.

page 57.   Old farm building, Dalfsen, The Netherlands. Dalfsen Photographers.

page 59.   P. J. Lloyd, "The Revolutionary War on the New York and Pennsylvania Frontiers." In Bruce Wilson, *As She Began* (Toronto: Dundurn, 1981), p. 38.

page 67.   Trade silver. Leonard Kroon.

239

page 69. B. Rawdon, "Col. Johnsons [sic] mounted men charging a party of British Artillerists and Indians at the Battle fought near Moravian Town October 2nd 1813 . . ." Print. Negative no. C7763. Picture Division, Public Archives of Canada.

page 71. "Allen Dolsen and Mrs. Roger Dolsen with Family Heirlooms." *Voice of the Kent Farmer.*

page 73. "The Dolsen Family Cemetery". *Voice of the Kent Farmer.*

page 75. J. C. H. Forster, "Encampment at Dolsen's Farm, Oct. 4, 1813". Watercolour, 1965. FF .77.19.1. Parks Canada: Fort Malden National Historic Park.

page 76. Harry Johnston, "The 'Devil' Visiting a Mandingo Town". Ibid., p. 78.

page 78. Harry Johnston, "Map of the Senegambia Region". In Harry Johnston, *Pioneers in West Africa* (London: Blackie, 1912), p. 118.

page 80. Harry Johnston, "The Fulas". Ibid., p. 250.

page 82. Harry Johnston, "Elephants Destroying a Palm Grove". Ibid., p. 86.

page 84. Artist unknown, "Tribal Prisoners of War". Print. Leddy Library, University of Windsor.

page 86. Artist unknown, "Captured Slaves". Print. Leddy Library, University of Windsor.

page 88. Artist unknown, "Plan of the Slave Ship *Brookes*, 1790". Print. Leddy Library, University of Windsor.

page 90. "The Petition of the Free Negroes to Simcoe, n.d." In Records of the Executive Council: Upper Canada, Land Petitions 1791-1817, RG 1 L3 Vol. 196 "F" Bundle Misc. file 68. Manuscript Division, Public Archives of Canada.

page 93. Philip Bouache, "A General Map of Senegal . . . 1756." In M. Adanson, *A Voyage to Senegal, the Isle of Goree, and the River Gambia* (London: J. Nourse, 1759).

page 96. Will of Richard Pawpine [sic] RG 22 6-2. Archives of Ontario.

page 99. H. Charles Devasagayam, "Ethnic Origins and Religious Groups, c. 1784". Manuscript Map, 1984 J. Magee.

page 100. "View from Riggisberg, Canton Bern". Elizabeth Magee.

page 102. "Parish Church, Thurnen, Canton Bern". Photo Studer, Thun, Switzerland.

page 104. "Interior of the Parish Church, Thurnen, Canton Bern". Photo Studer, Thun, Switzerland.

page 106. "Baptismal Font in Parish Church, Thurnen, Canton Bern". Photo Studer, Thun, Switzerland.

page 108. Emanuel Buechel, "Das Grossbasler Rheinufer". Etching, 1760. Public Art Gallery, Basel, Switzerland.

page 109. Artist unknown, "Rotterdam". Print. Gemeentearchief, Rotterdam, The Netherlands.

page 111. "Faiseur de Métier à bas". In Denis Diderot, *Enclopédie ou Dictionnaire raisonné des sciences, des arts, et des métiers* (Paris: Briasson, 1751-65), II. Plate 1.

page 114. Artist unknown, "Bostonians Paying the Exciseman, or Tarring and Feathering." Mezzotint, 1774. In James H. Stark, *The Loyalists of Massachusetts and the Other Side of the American Revolution* (Boston: James H. Stark, 1910), p. 49.

page 117. Richard Short, "Church of St. Paul and the Parade at Halifax, 1759". Drawing engraved by Jno. Fougeron, published by John Boydell, London, 25 April 1777. N-150. Public Archives of Nova Scotia.

page 121. "Mrs. George Moffat, née Anna Sophia Verge". c.1870. J. Magee.

240

# Index

244

245